Little Malcolm and his Struggle Against the Eunuchs

David Halliwell has worked as an actor, director and writer in theatre, radio, television and film since leaving RADA in 1961.

Little Malcolm and his Struggle Against the Eunuchs earned him the Evening Standard Most Promising Playwright Award. His other plays include: *A Who's Who of Flapland; Cock, Hen and Courtingpit; Bleats from a Brighouse Pleasureground; K. D. Dufford; A Last Belch for the Great Auk; Meriel the Ghost Girl; Creatures of Another Kind* (which won the John Whiting Award); *The House; Was It Her?; Bedsprings; Spongehenge; Tom in Pan and Pam in Tom; Parts; The Cutteslowe Walls; There's a Car Park in Witherton; Crossed Lines;* and *Bird*.

DAVID HALLIWELL

Little Malcolm and his Struggle Against the Eunuchs

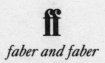

faber and faber

First published in 1967
by Faber and Faber Limited
3 Queen Square London WC1N 3AU

Photoset by Parker Typesetting Service, Leicester
Printed in England by Mackays of Chatham plc, Chatham, Kent

A CIP record for this book
is available from the British Library
ISBN 0-571-19670-5

2 4 6 8 10 9 7 5 3 1

Characters

Malcolm Scrawdyke
John 'Wick' Blagden
Irwin Ingham
Dennis Charles Nipple
Ann Gedge

Little Malcolm and His Struggle Against the Eunuchs was first performed at the Unity Theatre, London, on 30 March 1965. It was presented by Dramagraph and the cast was as follows:

Malcolm Scrawdyke David Halliwell
Irwin Ingham Michael Cadman
John 'Wick' Blagden Philip Martin
Dennis Charles Nipple Ron Cream
Ann Gedge Julian Burbury

Director and Designer Mike Leigh
Stage Manager Mo Race
Assistant Stage Manager Anne Marie Boxall

The play was subsequently presented by Michael Codron at the Gaiety Theatre, Dublin, for the Dublin Theatre Festival in September 1965; and the first performance at the Garrick Theatre, London, was on 3 February 1966. The latter was directed by Patrick Dromgoole and designed by Timothy O'Brien. The cast was as follows:

Malcolm Scrawdyke John Hurt
Ingham Rodney Bewes
Wick Kenneth Colley
Nipple Tim Preece
Ann Susan Ashworth

The play was revived by Hampstead Theatre and
presented on 12 November 1998 with the following cast:

Malcolm Scrawdyke Ewan McGregor
Ingham Nicholas Tennant
Wick Joe Duttine
Nipple Sean Gilder
Ann Gedge Lou Gish

Director Denis Lawson
Designer Rob Howell
Stage Manager Jane Erridge
Lighting Designer Johanna Town
Sound Designer John A. Leonard for AURA

*Light slowly comes up on the studio, 3A Commercial
Chambers. A grey, wan, wintry light. The room is large
and bleak. Upstage is a large deep window. The walls are
drab although paint of different colours has been daubed
on parts of them. Where there is no paint the colour is a
dirty, dingy grey-brown. The floor is of bare grey planks.
An upstage recess contains a sink. In the stage left wall is a
door, and more or less opposite it, in a shallow chimney
breast, is a very small gas fire and nearby a gas ring.*

*Over towards the door there is a single bed covered in
scruffy blankets. A couple of easels stand in the room, on
one of which there is a largish, unfinished, self-portrait of
Scrawdyke. There is a rickety table. There are two
nondescript wooden chairs, a battered armchair, a wooden
chair with arms and a high back. Scrawdyke's chair. A
couple of old tea chests, a large solid old radio cabinet,
and a dustbin. There is a record player on the table and a
tape recorder somewhere about. To one side there is a
large drum with Paramount Jazz Band roughly lettered on
it. Paintings on pieces of hardboard are stacked untidily
around the room and crockery, records, books, paper and
painting gear are littered about in every direction.*

*The general atmosphere is empty, squalid, damp and cold.
Malcolm Scrawdyke, a man of twenty-five, with long
hair and a beard, is sitting up in the bed, leaning back
against the end, with the clothes pulled up around him. He
looks balefully out at the scene.*

Scrawdyke Eeeeeeeergh! Toh . . . Faah . . . Get up. (*He*

I

doesn't move.) Come on get up! (*Doesn't move.*) Must be around two. Been lyin' 'ere an hour. Got t' get up. A'm starvin'. Look it's no use just theorisin' about getting up. It's the act 'at counts. Just a matter of makin' the decision. Exercise the will. The will! A'll count up t'five an' then the single decisive act. Right now. One . . . two . . . three . . . four . . . five. (*Doesn't move.*) Aaaargh! What is it determines the actual moment when – A mean A alwas do get up. Always manage it some'ow. What is it decides? 'Idden factor. Air currents? Vibrations? Oh 'oo the 'ell – 'Ow many times 'ave I been through all this without it ever makin' me get up when A say A will! The thing is t' creep up on y'self, tek y'self by surprise. Don't think. Suddenly. OK. Now! (*Doesn't move.*) Blast! All right. Now! (*This time he leaps out of bed. He is wearing a raggy black sweater, shirt and dark, scruffy jeans. He grabs a baggy, grubby jacket, puts it on.*) Done it! Done it! Done it! Self-mastery that's – Ooo 't's cold! Ooooooots! Where's me – (*Grabs large black overcoat off bed and scrambles into it.*) Aaah! Get it on yes what a life. Ugh. What a marvellous life for a man like me. (*Puts shoes on. He goes to the gas fire and turns the tap. No gas.*) Fah! (*Searches through pockets.*) Tanner – 'a'penny – what's – kopek! What the bloody use is – Oh no shillin'! No gas! No 'eat! 'Ave t' wait till those bastards get up 'ere. Where are they? (*Goes and looks out of window.*) Snow! January the first. What a – Put y' mark on this one, Malcolm, put y' mark on this one. (*Turns back into room.*) Fag. (*Fumbles one out.*) Give y' the shits first one but – (*Lights it.*) He could get out of bed at two o'clock, light up a fag, an' smoke it, just like that. What a man! (*Pacing around.*) Still A 'aven't started off too badly. Stirred up things down there. An' tonight's the night. 'Ow 'm I goin' to 'andle it? Won't be easy. But I've got t' really make that breakthrough. I know what I'm like but – This time, this time. Don't strain, take it easy. After all I know Ann's int'rested. She asked me. She asked me! That's a salient fact t' keep y'r sights on. All these months of scrapin' up excuses t' talk to 'er finally paid off.

'The's a film at the Empire A'd like t' see, what about . . .' No not 'What about', 'Would you'. Yes. 'Would you.' P'raps it's only the picture she's in'rested in. Oh don't be – Remember that tone. Yes this's my chance. Just take it easy.

Where the 'ell are they? Wonder what's goin' on down there? Chucked me out, the bastard. Just for 'avin a drag. No it wasn't – Culmination of five years arsin' around. Surprised 'e let me go on so long. Spent 'alf me bloody time down there sittin' in 'is room bein' given a last chance. If our positions 'ad been reversed I wouldn't 'ave tolerated 'im so long. 'The first day back, Scrawdyke, and I catch you in a petty infraction. You never learn, do you? Well this's the straw that breaks the camel's back. I'm going to start the New Year with a clean sweep. I'm kicking you out, Scrawdyke! That comes as a shock to you, doesn't it?' Well 'e was right, I never thought 'e'd do it. Why did I go there for a drag, near 'is door? That was a mistake. 'E's always touchy first few days back. I should'a' kept out of 'is way. Still I don't care, I wasn't goin' anywhere down there, I wouldn't 'ave passed Finals.

Fuck! Allard thinks e's finished me! But 'e's not 'eard the last. You may 'ave the first word, the second word, the third word an' the 'undred an' fifteenth word but I will 'ave the last word! What am A goin' t' do? Well – I'll make more trouble away from that place 'an I ever did inside it. Manipulatin' power from exile. Yeh I like that. Rule from afar, the gaunt, 'aggard, ghostlike exile, supposedly finished, forgotten. But all the time an unseen presence hauntin' from afar, pullin' 'idden strings. Ha! This's my Elba. Allard thinks 'e's got rid of me, but I live. What can I – Well, for a start I'll make sure Wick an' Irwin stay on that committee an' through 'em I'll – well I'll concoct something. Where the 'ell are they? (*He returns to the window and looks out, striking a slight pose.*) From out the snows he loomed, dark, wraithlike. A hollow menacing voice from the past.

Sounds of footsteps coming up the stairs. Scrawdyke turns. Ingham, wearing a donkey-jacket and baggy jeans, out of breath, bursts through the door.

Ingham I'm sorry, Mal.

Scrawdyke Where the hell 'ave y' been?

Ingham A'm sorry. Oh – uh, uh, A'm sorry, but well – uh uh, A've just run up 'ere.

Scrawdyke It 'asn't tekken y' two solid hours t' run up 'ere.

Ingham No, no, y're right. But y'see well like, y'see uh –

Scrawdyke What?

Ingham Yes. Well. Y'see – er, something 'appened.

Scrawdyke What?

Ingham Well, y'see like, this morning about 'alf eleven. All t' members o' t' committee like – Well, Allard called us to 'is room like. Me an' Wick an' Boocock an' –

Scrawdyke I know 'oo t' members o' t' committee are. I'm its chairman.

Ingham Aye, aye, right enough. Well, anyway, 'e gets us all in there like an' 'e explains like, well, 'ow 'e's 'ad t' ask you t' leave –

Scrawdyke Ask!

Ingham – an' 'e sez like 'e's called us in because we're t' committee of the Sketch Club an' 'ow as 'e 'as t' warn us –

Scrawdyke Warn you?

4

Ingham Aye, well y' know 'ow 'e – A mean, 'e sez you've been a disruptive influence – A mean that's 'is phrase – an' 'ow 'e's given y' chance after chance – A mean A'm not sayin' 'e's right A'm just tellin' y' what 'e said.

Scrawdyke Go on.

Ingham Yes, well, 'e goes on t' say 'at 'e doesn't like t'ave t' do it but 'e'll 'ave t' ask us, as sort of the representatives of the students like, not only not t' 'ave anything further t' do with y' ourselves like, but also t'go round all t'other students an' tell them as well. If, 'e sez, any student in future 'as anything t' do with y', meets y', talks t' y', an' 'e finds out like that they 'ave, 'e'll expel 'em immediately an' tell the education authorities t' stop their grants an' 'e'll make sure they don't get in t' any other art school. 'E sez if 'e doesn't do this like, an' your – influence isn't stopped – Well, the 'ole school might 'ave t' close down.

Scrawdyke smiling paces up and down.

Scrawdyke I'm not surprised, I'm not surprised. I could 'ave told y' this would 'appen. I could 'ave predicted it. 'E's shown 'imself in 'is true colours. Totalitarian, power mad!

Ingham Aye, well that's why A couldn't get up 'ere on time.

Scrawdyke It didn't tek 'im three hours t' tell y' –

Ingham No, no. Well afterwards like, we all, like, 'ad a bit of a –

Scrawdyke What did Wick say?

Ingham Ah well Wick. Well John – 'e said something more or less like you've just said.

Scrawdyke Boocock?

Ingham Well 'e seemed t' think like, 'at Allard might just, well 'ave gone just that little bit too far this time, 'e –

Scrawdyke Very radical of 'im. The balanced view. I hate intellectuals! An' what about Elaine Ackroyde an' that other emancipated beauty?

Ingham Ah well, the two girls, yes –

Scrawdyke What does that mean? 'Ah well the two girls yes.' What sort of a position is that?

Ingham No A di'n't mean that as their –

Scrawdyke Well, what did they say?

Ingham Well, Mal, y' know 'ow they sort of feel –

Scrawdyke That's all they can do, feel. An' what uncompromisin' position did you stoutly defend?

Ingham Well, I er – y' know I er, I could er – like, I er, well –

Scrawdyke What did y' say?

Ingham Well, A mean um, A can't exactly –

Scrawdyke What did y' decide t' do?

Ingham Ah well, Wick, 'e's got a plan.

Scrawdyke What?

Ingham Oh well, A think it's better if 'e like, tells y' 'imself when 'e gets 'ere.

Scrawdyke You tell me.

Ingham No, no, it'll be better if he –

Scrawdyke You don't agree with it?

Ingham Yes, yes, 'course A do. A mean Am' on your side, y' know that.

6

Scrawdyke Huh!

Ingham 'E'll tell y' when 'e gets 'ere.

Scrawdyke Well why isn't 'e 'ere now?

Ingham Ah well, y' see, that's all part of it.

Scrawdyke Keepin' me 'angin' around up 'ere, freezin', starvin'?

Ingham Av'n't y' 'ad owt t' eat?

Scrawdyke 'Ow could A? You were supposed to be bringin' me ten bob.

Ingham Oh aye, yes. (*Forks out ten-bob note.*)

Scrawdyke Ta. Y' av'n't got a shillin'?

Ingham Oh it's out. No.

Scrawdyke Well, give us a fag.

Ingham Yeh.

Scrawdyke Tipped!

Ingham Oh yeh.

Scrawdyke What the 'ell y' smokin' tipped for?

Ingham Well, y' see A pulled t' wrong thing on a machine.

Scrawdyke Contraceptives, I hate tipped. 'Ow's y' throat?

Ingham 'T's all right now.

Footsteps are heard rapidly coming up the stairs. Wick, dressed in a lumber jacket and narrow jeans, jumps in grinning.

Wick Aha there 'e is! Public Enemy Number One! (*Advances into room.*) Man y've done it this time! 'As Irwin told y'?

Scrawdyke 'E mentioned something.

Wick Yeh, well, when that little bastard got us in 'is room an' started on the big purge, I nearly burst a blood-vessel man! Mustn't see y', mustn't meet y', mustn't even mention your subversive name in those 'allowed attics. I couldn't believe me ears. I thought for a minute 'e was goin' t' order us all up t' t' Infirmary for blood tests and compulsory castration. It's the gas chambers for anybody 'oo even accidentally catches sight of a poor photograph of you mate.

Scrawdyke Y'd better start 'oldin' y' breath then.

Wick Aar! Y' don't think we're goin' t' tek any notice, do y'? A've never been so incensed! That little runt tellin' us 'oo we can see! An' afterwards those two chastity belts on legs, Ackroyde an' Firth, started on about it all bein' y're own fault. That little Ackroyde's really vicious when she gets goin'. She nearly clawed me eyes out when A said we should back you. Didn't she, Irwin?

Ingham Aye she nearly touched 'im.

Wick A'd 'ave touched 'er! I tried t' point out 'at Allard's tramplin' on our basic rights but there was no arguin' with 'em. An' Boocock was there in t' middle as usual, sayin' 'at although Allard's gone too far you 'ad ignored all 'is warnin's about skippin' classes, arsin' about, an' all that crap. An' of course, 'e didn't know what we ought t' do. Anyway I realized it was no good so Irwin an' me, we've worked out a little plan.

Scrawdyke Expatiate.

Wick Yeh. Look Allard thinks 'e's scared us off seeing you. 'E thinks we're so scared of missin' Finals an' not gettin' a plastic diploma we'll obey 'im. At least for a while, for a few weeks anyway. But even Allard can't

8

imagine we'll keep away from y' for ever. So all we've got t' do is wait. For a while we'll 'ave to play it cunnin'. What we'll do is this. Me and Irwin, we'll 'ave an arrangement with y'. We'll meet y' on certain nights, at certain pubs on the outskirts o' town. Y' know, a pub Monday, another for Tuesday, an' so on like that. Places where Allard can't possibly 'ave any spies. Say t' New Inn past Fartown, t' Clough 'Ouse up Fixby, some pub down Lockwood, out at Waterloo. We'll all go there separately an' we'll leave separately. Me an' Irwin 'ave already started, that's why we arrived 'ere separately. I ate in t' Tech canteen an 'e ate at Wrigleys –

Ingham Yeh.

Wick – an' we both came up 'ere by different routes an' we staggered our arrival. Anyway in future, if we pass y' on t' street, we won't even see each other, we'll cut each other dead. At least, that's what'll seem to 'appen. But actually we'll 'ave a secret little sign 'at'll be missed by even Allard's most observant 'enchlings. An infinitesimal twitch of the cheek, which'll mean, we're all t'gether, united, solid. It'll be so bloody subtle an' we'll be doin' it right under Allard's nose. 'E'll think 'e's won when all t' time the'll be this underground resistance. It'll be great! It'll be a conspiracy man! (*Pause.*) Well what d' y' think?

Scrawdyke glowers at them, moves, then looks at Wick.

Scrawdyke Phht!

Wick What's the matter with –?

Scrawdyke Gimme a fag.

Ingham Yeh, yeh.

Scrawdyke Not another o' those.

Ingham 'S all A've got.

Wick 'Ere A've got some Woodies.

Scrawdyke lights fag.

Scrawdyke You say that Allard'll think 'e's won. Well if we adopt your bold, darin' proposition, trudgin' miles through snow an' sleet t' remote, freezin' pubs for five minutes' furtive mumblin', sneakin' round town twitchin' our cheeks, of course Allard'll think that 'e's won. 'E'll 'ave ev'ry right t' think so. Because 'e will 'ave! It's exactly what 'e wants! I've never 'eard such complete an' supine capitulation masquerading as defiance. Allard did castrate you this mornin'.

Wick Look A'm just as disgusted by Allard as you are. 'Course we've got t' defy 'im. That's the 'ole bloody idea. But we've got t' play it cunnin'. Meet 'is blunt, naked force with subtlety. It's the only way.

Ingham Yeh.

Scrawdyke What a' you sayin' 'Yeh' for?

Ingham Well A mean –

Scrawdyke Y' don't mean anything, y' don't think anything an' y' never say anything. Y' never do. 'E's just t' same only 'e expresses it more fluently.

Wick Aw –

Scrawdyke What a pair you are! Allard insolently treats y' like mentally deficient hens and you boldly strike back by twitchin' y'r cheeks!

Wick I suppose you've got a better idea.

Scrawdyke I have. I always 'ave a better idea. Listen, this's a magnificent opportunity t' do all the things we've always talked about. Yesterday evening at eight twenty-five 'e threw me out. With reference to this I 'ave only one regret.

That I didn't walk out myself a year ago. Today 'e attempts to stifle your last vestiges of dignity. 'E threatens to expel you if you disobey 'im. Laugh in 'is face like free men an' leave!

Wick Leave?

Ingham But –

Scrawdyke Yes, leave, look the issue's simple. Freedom or serfdom. That's the choice. That's what it is. Surrender to 'im now and your integrity's gone, gone for all time. Whatever y' do in future y'll be utterin' empty noises, standin' on rotten boards. Y'll have betrayed y'selves, sold out, y'll be nothing but self-hatin' eunuchs. You'll know that when the critical moment rose up, you opted for nonentitihood. The choice you must make, an' it can't be shirked, is not just for today or tomorrow but for the rest of your lives. And what 'ave y' t' lose by leavin' now? A one-line question with a one-word answer. Nothing! Finals, NDD, what's that? Nothing! Nothing Doing Diploma which'll earn you the glorious privilege of designin' dogfood wrappers or keepin' a roomful of delinquents in order. Where's art in that? Where's life? Where's any form of tangible satisfaction?

John. You're the most talented painter 'oo ever walked through those dirty corridors an' attics down in that so-called School of Art. A man with your potential comes once in five generations, if that. They should be down on their knees begging, begging to help you. They should be overwhelmed with gratitude that they've been fortunate enough to earn footnotes in art history by 'elpin 'Uddersfield's one chance of puttin' a painter up there in the top rank alongside Cézanne, Matisse, Picasso. You are 'Uddersfield's Greatest Son and Allard treats you like a silly child. I know painting. I know your work. I say it is an outrage against the cultural aspirations of Mankind.

You know I don't say things like this lightly, I don't often turn my tongue to praise, I don't go around sprinkling confetti.

An' Irwin, you're a sensitive man, a man 'oo needs bringin' out, nurturin'. A magnificent draughtsman. The next Dürer. A man of profound depth. And what do they do down there? They crush y', whistle you around like a little dog. And what about women? Because you 'aven't got the small talk mentality, because you can't cavort, make with the easy flippant talk, they spurn you, snigger behind your back, don't even see you. They hand us nothing but contempt. Insults! Insults! Insults! Are we goin' t' go on takin' it for ever? Flat on our backs, with their farts in our faces! Is this the future y' see for y'selves? If it is then y're not the men I took y' for!

Wick No! Y're right! We can't let the buggers keep us down. When I think of all the guff I've taken from mediocrities! Man I'd like t' get back at 'em. I'd like t' show –

Scrawdyke Get your own back with a vengeance!

Wick Yeh.

Ingham Yeh, well, the's a lot in what y' – but, like, if we did, like, leave, A mean, y' say the's nothing down there, NDD. But what like could we do? An' then there's questions such as, well, like money, A mean . . .

Scrawdyke You're revellin' in theory, Irwin. Let's consider now the present concrete situation. Allard 'as issued a challenge. We must accept that challenge or resign all claim to being men. I face the challenge, I issue a retort. Don't go back to the Art School. Give it the two fingers. Let's form ourselves into a political party. We'll never 'ave a better opportunity and just think of the date. February the first. Man it's designed for such destinial action!

Wick Haha, yeh. Ey yeh, January the first!

Ingham But –

Scrawdyke Our first goal will be to smash Allard. Our ultimate goal'll be t' realize all our dreams, take our proper place in the scheme of things, an' achieve absolute power!

Wick Well it's an idea. Yeh! If we –

Scrawdyke 'If we'. What d'you mean, 'if we'? What 'ave we got t' lose? You agree there's no future bein' a cog in Allard's wheel.

Wick Yeh.

Scrawdyke So what do we lose?

Wick Nothing.

Scrawdyke Walk out. Think of the look on 'is face.

Wick Haha. Yeh.

Scrawdyke We've got the imagination and the will.

Wick Yeh. Come on let's do it! Let's make something 'appen. I'm sick of toein' the line, day in day out, in this provincial ghetto. We'll tell 'im where 'e gets off! What d'y' say, Irwin?

Ingham Oh but A mean . . . a Party.

Scrawdyke Well?

Ingham But A mean, a Party. The's only three of us.

Scrawdyke 'Itler started with seven

Wick An' Marx started with one, 'imself.

Scrawdyke Exactly.

Ingham But A mean, what could we do? A mean in 'Uddersfield?

Scrawdyke Just the place. The most unexpected quarter is just the place to launch a surprise offensive. Ev'ry strategist knows that.

Ingham An offensive? On what?

Scrawdyke The minds. The minds of the nation.

Wick We'll make this our 'eadquarters.

Scrawdyke Members'll come rollin' in.

Ingham Oh but A mean . . . we 'avent even got enough chairs.

Scrawdyke You're deceived by appearances, Irwin. You think because all you can see is three blokes in a drab room that's all there is. I see the reality; We are the germ. The revolution isn't in this room. It's up 'ere. Willpower. The first and last necessity. With it y' can do anythin', without it nothin'. An' we've got it.

Wick Because we're small now means nothing. A virus can kill – what? – an elephant.

Ingham But A mean 'oo's goin' t' – 'oo's goin' t' tek any – 'oo's goin' to join?

Scrawdyke Ultimately ev'rybody, whether they like it or not.

Wick Haha.

Scrawdyke . . . t' begin with kindred spirits. All over the country, on ev'ry street corner, the young an' frustrated are waitin'. They feel a deep resentment, a pent-up force. They don't know 'ow t' use it. They're tired of the old slogans. They yearn, they aspire, they wait for leaders. We are those leaders. We're here! They'll soon find out.

Wick Aye. And we shall –

Scrawdyke Of course we've got to start off with a concrete plan. We've got t' nobble Allard and do it in such a way that it's a symbolic gesture.

Wick Yeh what could we do?

Scrawdyke One decisive act. Don't theorize, do!

Wick What can we – it's got t' be –

Scrawdyke Well, are you with us?

Wick Are you goin' t' 'elp us get Allard?

Ingham Well –

Scrawdyke Are y' goin' to join us on the road to power?

Ingham Well, er –

Scrawdyke D' y' want it?

Ingham What?

Scrawdyke Power.

Ingham Er – er – er – uh – well – A wouldn't mind.

Wick Great! Three 'oo made a revolution!

Scrawdyke Two an' a third. Now we've got to find – we've got t' get Allard an' at the same time – a symbol. We've got t' astonish the world.

Wick Switch on a spotlight that'll illuminate –

Scrawdyke Of course the best thing'd be –

Wick What?

Scrawdyke . . . to kill 'im!

Wick Assassination!

Ingham Oh Mal, A mean –

Scrawdyke It's beautiful, it's simple, it's direct, an' above all it's violent.

Wick Clean an' decisive.

Scrawdyke But it could create sympathy for 'im.

Wick We've got to avoid that.

Ingham Aye, and we'd get sentenced to –

Scrawdyke There's something t' be said for the short jail sentence.

Wick Yeh, well A suppose it could make an impact.

Scrawdyke Yeh, quick martyrdom, couple o' weeks inside, then y're out t' pick up the sympathy.

Wick An' we needn't go in.

Scrawdyke 'Course not. We could let a comparatively inessential member take the rap. Whilst we, the real brains, exploit it outside. Irwin could go in.

Ingham Oh come off it, Mal.

Wick What's the matter? Y'd be a martyr, man! Y'd get all the glamour. Think of all the sympathetic birds comin' t' see y' on visitin' days.

Ingham Oh –

Scrawdyke 'Course y' wouldn't actually be able t' touch 'em.

Wick But think of all t' voluptuous dreams y' could 'ave in y' cell. The party in its munificence'd provide y' with a jockstrap free of charge. What an offer! The Movement's First Martyr. Y'd rank wi' Joan of Arc, man!

Ingham Not in a jockstrap A wouldn't.

They all laugh.

Wick Congratulations, Irwin. Sometimes –

Scrawdyke Yeh.

Wick gets out fags, hands them around.

So we rule out assassination.

Wick What about kidnappin' 'im?

Scrawdyke No, we've got t' show 'im up. Make 'im reveal 'imself for what 'e is. 'Ow? – 'Ow could we –

Wick Make 'im resign.

Scrawdyke – got to – first of all we've got t' get 'im. I know! We'll kidnap 'im.

Wick Great! Then do what?

Scrawdyke Er – Got it!

Wick
Ingham } What?

Scrawdyke Blackmail!

Wick Blackmail?

Ingham What wi'?

Scrawdyke What with! What with! Y've bin down in that art school four years an' y' don't know what with?

Ingham Well A mean like – 'e might be a bit unfair like but –

Scrawdyke Y're blind, Irwin! I saw it immediately. Margaret Thwaite!

Wick Margaret Thwaite?

Scrawdyke Margaret Thwaite.

Wick Margaret Thwaite!

Ingham Margaret Thwaite?

Scrawdyke Allard knocked 'er off!

Ingham Oh well A mean, 'e might 'ave necked with 'er a bit like at Chris'mas parties but –

Scrawdyke 'E did more than that.

Ingham What?

Scrawdyke 'E 'ad 'er in 'is car.

Ingham We've only 'er word for it.

Scrawdyke We've more than that. I've seen with me own eyes –

Wick I've seen 'er in that bloody car with 'im.

Ingham Well, I've seen her in 'is –

Wick Then 'ow can y' say we've only 'er word, then?

Ingham Well in 'is car, A mean what's that? Just a lift like, A mean we didn't actually see 'im, well y' know . . .

Scrawdyke She told me about it. I know the inside story. I make it my bizness t' ferret out these things. I'm not seduced by surface appearances. I never ignore the slightest scrap of seemingly irrelevant data. I keep my eyes skinned, I gather, I co-relate, I wait, an' then when I'm ready, I pounce! Allard knows that I know what there is t' be known. But 'e's 'ad t' move cannily . . . bide 'is time an' wait. To 'ave slung me out years ago would 'ave been too dangerous. I might 'ave spewed out the lot. So 'e's waited an' waited till the 'ole thing's receded into the past. I've been a marked man in that school for two years. Allard wears the mask of the artist, the guardian of sensibility, the up'older of good taste. 'E's considered fit t' guard an' guide young minds. But we all know that this mask is nothing but – a mask! Be'ind it cringes the real Allard, 'oo's int'rested in one thing an' one thing only –

18

Wick 'Is career.

Scrawdyke Power! We must strip the mask from the face of depravity. We must tear it away! Rip it! Smash it! Obliterate it! So that the world may stamp with both its feet on the insect beneath.

Wick What are we goin' t' blackmail 'im in t' doing?

Scrawdyke First things first. We've got t' let Allard know y've walked out.

Wick Yeh. Well what's the best way?

Scrawdyke Go and tell 'im.

Ingham Oh – can't we just like – send 'im a little note?

Wick Yeh. Maybe Irwin's got summat there.

Scrawdyke That's not leavin'; it's sneakin' out. I didn't send any notes.

Ingham Oh no, but like, 'e threw you out.

Scrawdyke That's what I let 'im think. I'd been waitin' for the right opportunity. If I'd just walked out any old time I'd 'ave put 'im on 'is guard.

Wick Ey, y' mean y' planned for 'im t' – ?

Scrawdyke I'm not sayin' I planned for it t' 'appen yesterday. That wouldn't be honest and A don't want to mislead y'. But y' know all the little things I've kept doin' t' niggle 'im. Well they weren't accidents. They seemed like accidents becos that's the way I wanted it. I knew 'at one time or another 'e'd catch me in some little infraction an' it'd incite 'im t' boot me out. That wasn't just an ordinary smoke I 'ad yesterday. It seemed like an ordinary smoke t' the unobservant eye but far from it. That smoke was worked out t' the last detail. Why d' y' think I went right into the corridor? Why d' y' think I went right up outside

19

'is door? If I'd just been after an illicit drag I could 'ave 'ad it in class be'ind that plaster cast.

Wick Aye y' could.

Ingham I thought y' went out there becos y' thought Allard was over t' road in pottery, an' like, y' didn't want t' leave smoke in t' room. A mean that's just what A thought.

Scrawdyke That's what you were intended t' think. I knew 'e was in 'is room, I've got a sixth sense for that man's movements. I didn't know whether 'e'd fall for it there and then, 'e might not see me or 'e might just warn me. But I knew 'at when 'e did fall for my little trap 'e'd follow it with all this purge stuff an' the scene'd be set for this. Was I surprised when y' told me?

Ingham Well – no – y' didn't seem –

Scrawdyke There you are. You'll take an ultimatum down telling 'im y've left.

Ingham An ultimatum!

Scrawdyke I'll write it for y'!

Wick Eh, what are we goin' t' call this party?

Scrawdyke Oh now, let's see – uh – it wants t' be – the Party of – Dynamic yes – I've got it – the Party of Dynamic Erection!

Wick Just the name!

Scrawdyke We're against the Eunarchy. We're against the castrated wherever they are. We're against all those 'oo want to reduce us to their level.

Wick Yeh. And when are we goin' t' stage the putsch?

Scrawdyke Now let's see – what is it today? Thursday, Friday tomorra. Give ourselves a week. We'll do it a week tomorra. We'll do it on Friday, January the ninth.

Wick Great! That will be the day! The Day of Dynamic Erection!

Scrawdyke The Day. The Day of Decision. The Day of Retribution. The Day of Will.

Wick The Day of Wrath. The Day of Truth.

Scrawdyke The Day of the New Fist.

Wick The First Day.

Scrawdyke The Last Day.

Wick The Birth Day.

Scrawdyke The Death Day.

Wick The Day of Iron.

Scrawdyke The Day of Steel.

Wick The Day of Aluminium.

Scrawdyke The Day of Molybdenum.

Wick The Day of Lead.

Scrawdyke The Day of Plastic.

Wick The Day of Mud.

Scrawdyke The Day of Porridge.

Wick The Day of Wet Cardboard.

Scrawdyke The Day of Horsehair Underpants.

Wick The Day of Chewed Grass Wigs.

They jump about with glee. They let out high-pitched yelps like dogs.

Blackout

SCENE 2

Scrawdyke bursts in. Switches on light. It is dark outside.
He bats snow off himself.

Scrawdyke Oooough! Sssss. Faah! No shillin'! Oh no 'eat,
no food, 'aven't eaten. Not even any comfort t' –

Oh, what a feeble – There it was all laid out an' I didn't,
I couldn't. Invites me down 'ome after – it's warm, it's
cosy, nobody about, gives me coffee. She lays back on the
sofa. I could even relax enough t' tek me coat off.
Stutterin', mumblin'. 'Well I er used t' drink more tea like,
y' know, than er I, er I, y' know like drink um coffee now.
A mean A've no real preference –' Wallpaper. Size of 'er
kitchen. Is it still snowin'? Anything but what I really
wanted. The way she sat on that sofa – the way 'er eyes.
Aargh, they mock me. So they should. What a spineless!
'Come an' sit down, Malcolm.' Oh stop it A can't stand it.
I perch there like a rigid board on t' end, she moves
slightly towards me and what did I do? Jumped up! She
wanted it, I know. An' I – What is this block? What is it?
Why am I so in'ibited? Why? Why me? All I want is t' be
treat like a 'uman being!

She told me about Irwin cowerin' outside Allard's office.
Allard comes out, Irwin just vaguely shoves t' ultimatum
at 'im an' scuttles away. She saw it. Wait until I –

Oh I talk about 'im. What about me!

I've 'ad it now. She'll never look at me again. That's
down the – what am I goin' to do? What am I going' t' do?
What!

I've got t' see 'er again!
Oh I can't 'ow could I –

Fix up a date! Phone 'er.

I'd never dare. I've never been able t' do things like that.
Write?

Oh she might show it 'er pals. They'd all giggle.

No she wouldn't, she's not like that.

After t'night she'll 'ave nothing but contempt.

No she'll think y' were just shy. Could be in y're favour.
Reserved. Not too fast.

But even if she does, 'ow can I see 'er?

An accident. Make it seem like an accident.

She'd see through it.

No she wouldn't. Not if y' worked it properly.

But 'ow?

Go to her place.

I couldn't. 'Ow'd that seem like an accident.

Say y' were just passin'. Say you'd been t' see Mick
Norris. 'E lives down that way.

But what if 'er mother's in?

She won't be. She works nights. Y' know that.

But I'd never dare knock. What'd I say?

You were just passin'.

I'd never get it out.

Repeat it over an' over again till it comes out automatic.
Chant it to y'self on y' way down there.

But even if A could. What when A get in?

The Party man. The bloody Party. That'll boost you in
'er eyes.

An' then what?

Well get 'er in the mood. Then, then – just throw y'self
in.

Oh it's impossible.

It's not.

It is.

It isn't.

It is.

You can.

23

I can't.

You can.

I can't.

You can.

I can't.

You can! Don't brood about after. Just get in. Get in. That by itself'll show 'er something. Even if y' don't get started this time y'll be keepin' the ball rollin'.

Well I –

What else is the' t' do?

Nothing.

Well do it!

When?

Tomorra night.

Not tomorra night. I need time.

It's got t' be. Y've got t' get in quick before it's too late.

Oh –

Y' c'n see that can't you?

I –

You can see it, can't you?

I suppose so –

Good!

What time?

She catches the nine o'clock trolley. Be down at 'er place at – ten.

'S too early. She'd suspect.

No, no, she won't know 'ow long y've been at Mick's – So y'll do it?

Yes. I'll try.

Not try. Do!

I'll do it. Yes. I'll do it. I'll – The Party.

Yes, that'll astound 'er. Oh if I can bring this off, fuck the Party. Ann'd be my real conquest; not all this Dynamic Nonsense.

Well I've got some action. Got people around me. That's something. I hate bein' all on me – All those years I lived

24

out in Bailiff Bridge, seven miles away, out on the edge, ev'ry weekend pinin' away in silence.

'Uddersfield's always been the centre t' me.

Came in ev'ry day t' conquer it. Along the spoke into the hub. An' all this time I've never felt – I still don't belong. Not my town. I'll make it my town! I'll make it sit up! I'll make the bloody world think I *am* 'Uddersfield. Inseparably linked, Scrawdyke, ah, yes, 'Uddersfield. Leavin' 'ome that was a good move. I'll get Wick and Irwin to move in 'ere. Then I won't be on me own. I'll get Ann. That'd be the biggest – Yes, I must act an' I must act now!

Ooo 't's so cold! Get t' bed! (*During the following he removes coat, puts it on bed, removes shoes.*) Got t' try an' sleep. If I could only sleep t'night. Blank mind. Secret of success 's a blank mind. Yes. Just lay there. Switch off – Ooo it's bloody cold! Well never – (*Switches light off. Blackout. Gets into bed.*) Friday, January the second now. This 's got t' be *the* year. Yes. Now come on relax, go blank. Then – the 'ole thing's – only a question of doin' it.

Lights up. Grey noonday light. Scrawdyke is sitting up in bed. Dennis Nipple, a tallish, slouching, lumbering man of twenty-six, in shabby duffle-coat, with the hood up, is standing.

Nipple Noe, no y' wrong.

Scrawdyke I'm tellin' t' it was green!

Nipple Noe it wasn't it was blue.

Scrawdyke It was green.

Nipple Noe blue.

Scrawdyke I should know, it was my jacket.

Nipple Well Ai saw it.

Scrawdyke You saw it! I wore it. For two years.

Nipple Noe not for so long.

Scrawdyke' Ow the 'ell d' you know?

Nipple Ai c'n remember.

Scrawdyke Y' timed it?

Nipple Noe, but A know it wasn't so long.

Scrawdyke You can't even remember the colour of it.

Nipple Ai can. It was a sort of dingy blue.

Scrawdyke It was a mellow green.

Nipple Noe y' can't call it green. Y' might say it 'ad a very slight greenish tinge, but it was blue.

26

Scrawdyke You obviously can't tell the diff'rence between blue an' green.

Nipple Noe it's you 'oo caan't tell the diff'rence. Y' call y'self an artist an' y' can't –

Scrawdyke I know that jacket. You're colour blind. Y've got a very poor visual sense. Words are your medium.

Nipple That may be. But A'm sensitive t' colour an' shade. Ai caan't paint but Ai c'n see.

Scrawdyke Then why d' y' wear them thick specs?

Nipple They don't stop colours comin' through. They intensify.

Scrawdyke They blur and distort.

Nipple Noe, you're just makin' excuses for y'r own lack of observation.

Scrawdyke Look, when a man wears a jacket for two blasted years 'e ought t' know what colour it is.

Nipple Noe, yoo mustn't ever 'ave looked at it, Ai suppose, y' were too deep in intellectual thought as usual. Yoo don't notice what goes on around y'. Ai do. Ai've got a keen perception for the world of the senses. Sights, sounds, odours, tactile titillations. I'm a walking seismograph of sensual innuendo. A feast on 'em. They're the raw stuff from which Ai weave.

Scrawdyke Balls! Y' can't see six inches in front of y' face. Y' couldn't smell a roomful of dead elephants. If a time-bomb went off in y're pocket – Oh I'm not goin' t' argue with y'. This nonsense about the jacket shows 'ow perceptive you are.

Nipple Now y' just tryin' t' – It's yoo 'oo's unperceptive. Only yoo could even imagine it was green.

Scrawdyke Listen, mate. I'll tell y' 'ow unperceptive you are. If that jacket 'ad a tendency towards any other colour than green, it was brown.

Nipple Oh noe. Ai admit it wasn't pure blue. There was an 'int of green, just an 'int. But A don't know where y' get brown from.

Scrawdyke An 'int of green. It was green! Green with a tendency towards brown.

Nipple Ai never saw any brown.

Scrawdyke You wouldn't. You only see what y' want to.

Nipple Ai saw it as blooey green.

Scrawdyke Listen that sort of corduroy jacket mellows with wear, with the weather on it, an' the green takes on a –

Nipple It wasn't corduroy.

Scrawdyke Of course it was corduroy.

Nipple Nah, nah, it were a sort of stuff made up t' look like corduroy.

Scrawdyke It was the real thing. 'Ow the 'ell would you know?

Nipple Noe real corduroy's not like that. Y' c'n tell if y' see real corduroy. Y' c'n tell, it's a subtle diff'rence. It 'as a richer sort o' texture.

Scrawdyke It was bought as corduroy. I should know.

Nipple Hee, hee, y' were taken in.

Scrawdyke I was not taken in. I know corduroy. I asked for a corduroy jacket an' that's what I got.

Nipple Noe yoo can't afford reel corduroy.

Scrawdyke It 'ad the bloody label in it.

Nipple Oh well Ai suppose they called it corduroy. A mean that's 'ow they sell it t' people like you. But Ai –

Scrawdyke So you can discern that a jacket isn't corduroy, even if it looks like corduroy, feels like corduroy, an' is called corduroy. You 'ave a mystical sixth sense for the real corduroy.

Nipple Noe but Ai c'n tell. Yoo're not clo'es conscious like me.

Scrawdyke I know clothes. I don't dress by accident. I choose my outfit with care. I reject fashionable elegance. I present an image, haggard, gaunt, unkempt. I dress with style.

Nipple Hee hee after the Revolution ev'rybody 'll 'ave t' dress like yoo. It'll be the 'ight of fashion. Hee hee. An' mai books'll be made compulsory readin'.

Scrawdyke You'll allow your work to be published? A thought that was beneath your dignity?

Nipple Noe, noe, Ai never said that. Ai said 'at public honours 'old no temptation for mee. The reel writer, the great writer dismisses prizes an' honours as unworthy of 'im. The only tribute 'e accepts is the readin' of 'is work. 'E stands alone, remote. A great crag risin' out of the plain of ordinariness.

Scrawdyke Where the 'ell's Irwin with those chips A sent 'im for?

Nipple Where's 'e gone for 'em?

Scrawdyke That place up there, just opposite.

Nipple South Parade.

Scrawdyke No that street just opposite. Y' c'n see it through t' winder.

Nipple That's South Parade. (*Nipple moves to window, looks out.*)

Scrawdyke It's not.

Nipple It is. They've put cinders down on Chapel 'Ill.

Scrawdyke I know that.

Nipple All is crowned in white. T' roofs o' those shops opposite. Even t' Public Bog over there is mantled with flaky ermine. That letter box at t' bottom of South Parade –

Scrawdyke It's not called South Parade.

Nipple It is.

Scrawdyke Oh well A'm not goin' t' argue with y'. Y're disputatious. I 'av'n't 'ad owt to eat for forty-three hours.

Nipple Once Ai went for longer 'an that without food.

Scrawdyke When?

Nipple Last summer after that party at Barry Lawton's when me mother locked me out by mistake. Ai decided t' see 'ow long A could go without food an' sleep. Ai decided t' seek the unknown vistas of the 'allucinated mind. Ai embarked on a pilgrimage to the dream city of surreal experience. Ai wanted t' see if Ai could induce 'allucinations.

Scrawdyke Your 'ole life's an 'allucination.

Nipple Noe, noe, let me tell y'.

Scrawdyke I wouldn't dream of stoppin' y'.

Nipple Ai came into town an' as Ai walked about Ai fell

into a trance. Ev'rything Ai encountered took on a new
shape, a new form, a new meanin' – Ai seemed t' float
through the streets. The crowds loomed past me like crazy
phantoms. The girls in their summer frocks were like
diaphanous chatterin' birds ready t' take wing an' soar
through the air. The trolley-buses floated, suspended, great
red toys glidin' nowhere, 'ither and thither, to an' fro –
Their 'uman cargoes no more than playthings. The 'ole
scene no more than a surreal kaleidoscope pageant of
insubstantial seemin'. Hee, hee – Then Ai went down Leeds
Road t' the Gas Works, just t' look at it, just t' experience it.
Ai stood there an' it rohze before me. Shimmerin' –
Pulsatin' – Its chimneys became dark minarets against the
'azy blue canopy of the 'eavens. Its gasometers were – were
'eavin' symbols of dark leashed power. Its coolin' towers
were soarin' mirage palaces, leapin' t' block out the life-
givin' light. An' the 'ole mesmeric vision belched an' fumed
its noxious vapours. A cathedral dedicated to evil. The very
ground trembled. Ai felt asphyxiated. The spittle dried in
mai throat. Ai choked an' gasped in vain. The terrible,
ghastly, impingin' vision clawed at me tryin' t' drag me in.
With overwhelmin' force it sucked at me. Suckin' me t'
destruction! With a last utter, final frenzy Ai managed to –
turn an' stagger away. (*Pause.*)

Scrawdyke It's a terrible place, that Gasworks. T' Council
should be told about it.

Nipple, still entranced, doesn't reply.

If that's what it does to innocent young mystics they
ought to put a screen round it.

Nipple Hee hee.

*Wick and Ingham come in. Ingham is carrying
Scrawdyke's chips. They both raise their arms and give
the salute – Ingham also raises the chips.*

Wick
Ingham } Hail Scrawdyke!

Scrawdyke salutes from bed.

Scrawdyke Hail Scrawdyke! Where did y' go for these chips – Heckmondwyke?

Ingham No. A went up South Parade.

Nipple Hee hee.

Wick Aha Nipple. The Greatest Sucker of 'em all.

Scrawdyke gets up and puts his jacket, coat and shoes on.

Nipple Oh don't start crackin' all those corny –

Wick So y' don't like my gags?

Nipple They're in bad taste.

Wick What could be in better taste than a Nipple? (*Makes a sucking shape with his lips.*)

Nipple Waah, that's not funny.

Scrawdyke Get on wi' that banner.

Ingham starts working.

Wick Sorry A'm late, Mal.

Nipple Ai suppose that was the party salute?

Wick Ey! Does 'e –?

Scrawdyke I've appointed 'im the Party Archivist an' Minister of Records. We need an 'istorian on the spot from the word go.

Wick Oh yeh.

Nipple That's not a proper salute.

Wick It's a perfectly good salute.

Nipple Noe, no, y' shouldn't bend y'r arm like that. Y' should raise it like this.

Wick You're findin' a lot of fault, Nipple. It's an honour t' be invited t' join this Party, especially at this early stage.

Nipple Ai don't see –

Scrawdyke Look, either you accept my authority, an authority unanimously vested in me, or y' c'n push off.

Nipple Waaarh.

Wick Well?

  Nipple shuffles.

Nipple – awright?

Wick All right what?

Nipple All right Ai agree.

Wick Raise y' right arm like this.

  Nipple does.

Do this with y' fingers.

Nipple Waagh, it makes it look as though y' tryin' t' grasp something.

Wick We *are* tryin' t' grasp something y' silly bastard. Now repeat after me. I Dennis Nipple.

Nipple That's not mai name.

Wick Then what is y'r name?

Nipple Dennis Charles Nipple.

Wick OK, I Dennis Charles Nipple.

Nipple Ai Dennis Charles Nipple.

Wick On this second day of January.

Nipple Is that the right date?

Wick Of course it is!

Nipple Wait a minute it's not. It's the third t'day.

Scrawdyke It's the bloody second. Get on with it!

Wick On this second day of January.

Nipple Oh well, it's your mistake. On this second day of January.

Wick Swear an oath of personal allegiance to my Leader Malcolm Scrawdyke.

Nipple Swear an oath of personal allegiance to the Leader Malcolm Scrawdyke.

Wick And through absolute obedience to his will to the aims and struggle of the Dynamic Erectionist Party.

Nipple And through absolute obedience to 'is will to the aims an' struggles of the Dynamic Erectionist Party.

Scrawdyke has finished his chips. He puts on a record of Tommy Ladnier.

Scrawdyke I've been thinkin'. We need a new calendar. This is the New Year One, an' we need new names for the months.

Wick Yeh, that's a great idea, man.

Scrawdyke All the old names are after Roman Gods. We're openin' up a new Pantheon.

Wick We'll give 'em our names.

Scrawdyke Exactly. January, the first month, becomes the month of Scrawdyke, February becomes Blagden, March, Ingham, an' April Nipple.

Wick Oho, Nipple. We can't call a month Nipple. Y'll have t' change y' name.

Nipple Ai'm not changin' mai name.

Wick All y' need's a pseudonym – Papworthy, Titteringham.

Nipple Noe.

Wick Dennis Erotogenic-hyphen-Zone.

Nipple Ai'm not ashamed of mai name.

Scrawdyke It'll soon lose its 'umorous connotations when we come to power.

Wick Anybody found smilin' durin' the month of Nipple will be arrested immediately on a charge of insolence. The next eight lucky beggars 'oo join this party get a month named after 'em. What other movement can offer a similar incentive?

Scrawdyke I've thought of another thing. We must 'ave a magazine. An official organ.

Wick With a name like Dynamic Erection we can't do without it. What about callin' it Hard Facts.

Scrawdyke Yeh. No I've thought of a name – the Muckshifter.

Wick Just the job.

Nipple No, y' don't want a name like that. It's too mundane. Y' want something with an aura, something upliftin' spiritual.

Scrawdyke That's its name and you're its editor.

Nipple Waah.

Scrawdyke Now let's get on with plannin' the putsch.

Wick Right. Now next Friday, Scrawdyke the ninth, we're goin' to whip a paintin' from t' Art Gallery. We're goin' t' bring it 'ere, right? Then later in t' evening' we're goin' t' kidnap Allard an' blackmail 'im int' smashin' t' paintin'. We're goin' t' say smash it or we'll spill the beans about Margaret Thwaite. 'E'll smash it and then we'll shout it to the world!

Scrawdyke An' that my friends will be our lever to everlastin' fame. Now t' first part, t' first phase of the operation 'll be the raid on t' Art Gallery. (*Scrawdyke goes and switches the record off.*) Now let's work this out. Come on, Irwin. Right so we arrive at the entrance. Come on Irwin.

They start to act it out.

Wick Right. So we're in the entrance 'all.

Scrawdyke We look around.

Wick The's an old bird comin' out o' t' library.

Nipple The's somebody comin' down t' stairs.

Scrawdyke Ignore 'em. Walk casually t' the lift.

Wick 'Oo's got t' portfolio?

Scrawdyke Irwin. (*He gets it.*)

Ingham Oh ta.

Nipple The lift's got somebody in it.

Scrawdyke No it 'asn't.

Nipple It 'as!

Scrawdyke No it 'asn't! It's never used at this time.

Wick Well if it 'as we walk up.

Scrawdyke Emergency plan.

36

Wick Aye. We get in the lift.

They squeeze together in a tight square.

Scrawdyke Come on. Now I'm nearest the button.

Nipple No Ai'm nearest the button.

Scrawdyke Which side is it?

Ingham Er – that side.

Scrawdyke Then move over.

Nipple Ai don't see –

Scrawdyke I press the button.

Nipple Oh.

Scrawdyke Right. We're on our way up.

Wick Zzzzzzzzzzzzzzzzzzzzzzz –

Nipple Why –

Scrawdyke Shh! No talkin'! We're there.

Wick Open t' gates.

Scrawdyke Out.

Wick Come on, Irwin!

Ingham Oh aye yeh.

Scrawdyke Quick look round.

Wick An' we go through the turnstile.

Scrawdyke Good we're in. T' modern stuff's in this first gallery.

Wick There's somebody down t' far end!

Nipple Ai don't see anybody.

Scrawdyke That's becos y're 'alf blind. Disperse, look casual, go on, Irwin, look at that – look at that Sutherland.

Ingham Er – where is it?

Wick Down there by t' sink.

Ingham Oh.

Wick I'll go up near t' entrance.

Nipple looks at Scrawdyke's self-portrait.

Nipple Hee hee. Ai'll look at this thing.

Scrawdyke Don't be funny. Get down there. Just up from Irwin. An' be casual.

Nipple Waah.

Scrawdyke An' I'll look at this wall. (*Pause*)

Wick They've gone!

Scrawdyke Action stations! Wick cover t' entrance. Nipple you watch t' exit at t' other end. Go on, get a move on. Irwin you come t' me wi' t' portfolio. We go t' t' Spencer, which is on this wall.

Nipple No it's not there.

Scrawdyke 'Course it is. That's where it 'angs, on this wall.

Nipple Noe it's down 'ere on this wall.

Wick Wait a minute, Mal, 'e may be right.

Scrawdyke I know where it is.

Nipple It's over there.

Wick A'm not sure but A think it's down 'ere.

Scrawdyke No.

Wick Irwin.

Ingham Well er like, A'm not sure, A'm not sayin' 'at anybody's really er – y' know, like – A mean A don't want t' be dogmatic –

Scrawdyke Come on, man! Ev'ry second counts!

Ingham Well t' t' best of me er – A seem t' remember like, 'at it's on that wall where you are, Mal.

Scrawdyke Where?

Ingham Er – a bit further up like, no, no, up that way.

Scrawdyke Right. Come on. Keep watch. OK. I-lift-it-off-its-'ooks-an' slowly, slowly, gently bring-it-down. 'Old the bag open. Ease it in. Got it.

Ingham drops portfolio.

Don't let it go!

Ingham Oh – sorry.

Wick We look around. T' attendant's comin'.

Scrawdyke He isn't. Irwin get in t' lift wi' t' paintin'. Wick you with 'im.

Wick Fine.

Scrawdyke Nipple, you an' me'll saunter casually down t' stairs. We all meet at t' bottom.

Wick Right. Zzzzzzzzzzzzzz –

Scrawdyke Right off we go.

They walk side by side, round and round the other two.

Nipple Noe it's not. Yoo don't know 'ow t' saunter. This's a saunter.

Scrawdyke I saunter in my own way.

Nipple Nobody'd guess. Noe this's a saunter.

Scrawdyke That 'eavy, clumpin' torpor.

Nipple Well it's better'n what yoo're doin'. Y' like a jerkin' spastic.

Scrawdyke Ask anybody what I'm doin' an' they'd tell y' I'm saunterin'. Ask 'em what you're doin' an' they'd be 'ard pressed t' tell y' were movin'.

Wick – zzzzzzz!

Nipple The's nothin' wrong with the way Ai walk.

Scrawdyke 'Ow would you know, y've never done any.

Nipple Aar, yoo 'ave no grace in y' movements.

Scrawdyke Of course I 'ave. I know 'ow t' saunter.

Nipple Noe.

Scrawdyke This's the essence of saunterin'.

Nipple Noe, that's not saunterin'.

Wick Ey, 'ow long is it goin' to tek you two t' saunter down 'ere? We've bin 'ere ten minutes. Shall we go up an' down again t' give y' time?

Scrawdyke No we're there.

Wick Right. Out we get.

Ingham Ee A've got cramp standin' still like that.

Wick The's a point there, Mal, we sh'll get down 'ere before you. We can't 'ang around.

Scrawdyke Exactly, I've foreseen that.

Nipple Then why did y' 'ave 'em goin' down before us then?

Scrawdyke As soon as y' get t' t' bottom get out. Irwin goes out immediately wi' t' portfolio. You say 'Goodbye' to 'im, 'See y' tomorra.' 'E goes out. You make sure nobody follers 'im, then just stroll out.

Wick Can't I saunter?

Scrawdyke If y' know 'ow. Irwin you walk down t' steps, fairly quickly, but don't run, just a nice brisk walk, an' make y' way 'ere. Now, Wick, you foller 'im out, y' can watch 'im safely across Ramsden Street out o' t' corner of y'r eye.

Wick Yeh.

Scrawdyke Then make y' way t' t' Gates café. Me an' Nipple'll foller y' at a distance, casually, an' join y' there. We'll 'ave a cup o' tea an' we'll keep a lookout through t' winder.

They sit down.

Wick We'll be able t' see Irwin when 'e turns t' corner of East Parade an' goes in t' studio. Triumph.

Scrawdyke But we mustn't show it.

Wick No play it dead cool, man.

Scrawdyke We mustn't mention it. Talk about something else.

Wick Is pickin' one's nose a venial or a mortal sin? If one postulates the Deity as a Super Stick Insect where does that place the average man?

Scrawdyke We sup up. Come on 'ere, an' that's it.

They get up.

Wick In the bag!

Scrawdyke The first phase completed.

Wick Gone without an 'itch.

Scrawdyke We've done it!

Wick shakes hands with Scrawdyke.

Wick Congratulations.

Scrawdyke Well done!

They all shake hands with each other.

Nipple Hee hee.

Scrawdyke Well done, Irwin.

Ingham Oh – well – ta.

They walk round each other, shaking hands, patting one another on the back.

Wick Master stroke.

Scrawdyke Well done, lads.

Nipple Hee hee.

Scrawdyke Great, great.

Wick Went like clockwork.

Scrawdyke Yeh.

The congratulations peter out. They are left standing there. Pause.

Wick It'll be a doddle.

Scrawdyke Without question. Right. Now we've got the paintin' 'ere we move on t' t' next phase.

Wick Gettin' Allard!

Ingham 'Ow d' y' suggest we do that?

42

Nipple Put 'im in a taxi.

Scrawdyke Got it! 'Is own car! (*Pulls bed into position for car.*) Right we wait be'ind the fence 'ere. Just by the gap. Allard's car's parked just along, there.

Wick We wear masks. (*Gets out handkerchief.*) Round our mouths.

Scrawdyke hasn't got a hanky. He finds a brightly coloured bit of rag.

Ingham I 'aven't got a –

Scrawdyke Use a rag then.

Ingham Oh yeh.

Nipple Where's one for me?

Scrawdyke I don't know – use that.

Nipple Err, this?

Scrawdyke Yes, get it on.

Nipple Errgh, it's somebody's mucky old vest.

Scrawdyke Well get it on!

Nipple I'n't there anything else?

Scrawdyke Stop quibbling an' get it on.

Nipple Waargh.

Wick So we're in be'ind the fence.

Scrawdyke Yes. Come on, Nipple.

Nipple Aar A c'n 'ardly breathe in this smelly thing.

Wick It's great. It looks very sinister.

Scrawdyke We've all got sticks.

He grabs sticks, bits of wood, and hands them out.

Right, now Allard comes out of the buildin'.

Wick runs off to be Allard, pulling off the handkerchief, dropping stick.

We wait, just by the openin' in the fence, like a coiled spring ready t' pounce.

Wick Allard comes out of the Tech. Just as 'e always does. Feelin' cheerful an' a little tired, thinkin' about 'is supper, 'is wife, an' 'is bed.

Scrawdyke 'Ummin' to 'imself. Lookin' forward to a nice drive 'ome through the snow.

Wick Thinkin' about all the little things 'at 'ave 'appened durin' the day. The little kicks. When 'e told a joke in the staff room, the warm feelin' 'e got when ev'rybody chuckled. The little annoyances 'e's 'ad like catchin' students chuckin' clay at the model.

Scrawdyke But all in all it's been a good day.

Wick An unexceptionable day.

Scrawdyke But a good day.

Wick starts walking, humming to himself.

· **Wick** 'E walks down the side of the Tech. Turns the corner into St Paul's Street.

Scrawdyke Goes past the gap an' gets to 'is car.

Wick 'E gets out 'is keys.

Scrawdyke Bends down to open the door. We come out, quickly, from the darkness, silently.

Wick starts to unbend but they are on him. Scrawdyke leading. They rain pretend blows down on him. After

44

*the initial few blows all the assailants seem to get carried
away by what they are doing: Wick lets out muffled
gasps and groans. Finally Wick lies inert. Scrawdyke
gives him a final kick and they have finished.*

Nipple Ah, ah, we've killed 'im, hee, hee.

Scrawdyke No! Get 'im in the car.

*They seize hold of Wick and heave him into the 'back
seat'.*

Irwin, the wheel, Nipple in the back.

Scrawdyke sits beside Ingham.

Start 'er up!

Ingham Oh – er – well.

Scrawdyke Ignition!

Ingham Oh yeh.

Wick raises himself up.

Wick Are we goin' to reverse?

Ingham Oh look, A mean, let's not.

Scrawdyke No attract too much attention. Straight on St
Paul's.

Wick Mmmmmmmmmmmm . . .

Nipples Stop at the end.

Scrawdyke Straight round the corner.

Wick Mmmmmm, up past Sparrer Park, Mmm . . .

*When he isn't speaking and the car is moving Wick
makes the Mmmm noise.*

Scrawdyke Stop at the traffic lights.

Nipple There aren't any traffic lights there.

Scrawdyke There are.

Wick Crash straight ahead through 'em.

Scrawdyke Too risky.

Nipple They've changed.

Scrawdyke Not yet – They've changed!

Wick Straight up Ramsden Street.

Scrawdyke Yeh.

Wick Up t' the top.

Scrawdyke No not up t' t' main street. Too many people. Turn on Peel Street.

Nipple Hee hee, past t' Police Station.

Wick No we don't want that. Reverse.

Ingham Ooh!

Wick Reverse, Irwin, quick, quick. The's a cop lookin' at us.

Scrawdyke Back int' Ramsden Street again.

Nipple Which way a' we goin'?

Wick Back down t' t' crossroads an' on Queen's Street.

Scrawdyke No, no. That's past Tech. They'll all be comin' out.

Wick We'll 'ave t' go back then, back t' St Paul's an' go on the other way.

Scrawdyke Back where we started!

Ingham No, no the's another little street like off Ramsden Street, top side o' t' Town 'All, A don't know its name.

Nipple Aye there is. Back o' Whitfields shop.

Scrawdyke On there then.

Wick Not many about.

Nipple Their dark car speeds through unknowin' snowflaked streets of night.

Scrawdyke Turn down Princess Street.

Wick Then on Alfred Street.

Scrawdyke Then up East Parade.

Wick Look out for that lorry! Skreeetch! Phew! That was a close one!

Nipple Door's come open.

Scrawdyke Close it!

Wick Allard's fallen out!

Scrawdyke Can't 'ave. Round the corner. Pull up. (*Short pause.*)

Wick Man what a ride!

Scrawdyke OK now is there anything about?

Nipple The's a trolley comin' up Chapel 'Ill.

Scrawdyke Never mind. We'll get 'im out. It's only a couple o' yards in t' t' buildin'. If anybody interferes we'll say 'e's drunk.

Wick My father, madam. Don't y' think it's amazing I've turned out so well? (*He lies down.*)

Scrawdyke All right get 'old of 'im. That end Irwin, come on.

Nipple Ai want to take me rag off.

47

Wick Don't be disgustin'.

Scrawdyke Right, get 'im upright. Under 'is arms, come on. Across the pavement. Ugh. An' in at the door. Now we've got t' get 'im up these bloody stairs.

Wick Well look we've got the real stairs just outside. Why don't we –

Scrawdyke Aye. Good idea. Come on.

They all go out of the door and close it behind them. We can only hear them. They run down to the bottom of the stairs.

Wick Oo, still showin'! Man, it's cold!

Scrawdyke Right get 'old of 'im again. Other side Nipple. Irwin what a' you doin'?

Ingham Be'ind.

Scrawdyke OK let's – ugh – Come on! Push, Irwin.

Ingham I am.

Nipple Yoo're not takin' enough weight.

Scrawdyke I am, you aren't.

Nipple Ai can't take any more.

Scrawdyke 'Course y' can.

Nipple Yoo don't know 'ow t' lift.

Scrawdyke I'm bearin' the brunt. Anybody c'n see you've never carried –

Nipple Now, y've got y' arms all wrong. They should be like this.

Scrawdyke Don't let go! Aargh! Y've pinned me against the wall, y' silly bastard!

Nipple Noe Ai 'av'n't, you've done it.

Wick Wait a jiff. A'll stand on me own weight a bit.

Scrawdyke Oh! Right, get 'im, under this way.

Nipple Noe y' can't.

Scrawdyke Do as y' told.

Nipple It's not –

Scrawdyke Shurrup and lift.

Measured tread of somebody descending stairs from above studio. Ingham whispers.

Ingham The's somebody comin'!

They talk urgently in whispers. Measured tread continues down.

Wick From t' top floor!

Ingham Go back down.

Scrawdyke No stay as we are.

Nipple 'E won't be able t' get past.

Scrawdyke Yes 'e c'n squeeze, press against the wall.

Nipple But what –

Scrawdyke Shhh!

Footsteps continue, then stop as Wick says:

Wick Huh, slipped outside, sprained me ankle.

Scrawdyke 'E'll be all right when we get 'im inside.

Wick Yeh, just twisted it really – huh.

Pause. Footsteps start down again.

49

Scrawdyke Come on, lads, let's get 'im up there. Not far now. Lift, Nipple.

Nipple Ai am.

Scrawdyke Nearly – Ugh – just a bit –

Door opens. They come in lugging Wick. Scrawdyke at one side, Nipple at the other, Ingham behind.

Put 'im on t' bed.

They get him on to the bed,

'E was a weird bloke. Never said anything, just stared. What was the matter with 'im? We told a plausible story, did it convincingly. Most people would 'ave sympathized. 'E was an odd bastard. What – Tah! The masks! We still 'ad the bloody masks on!

Wick laughs on bed.

Nipple Aar yoo ought to 'ave thought of that.

Scrawdyke What about you? You didn't realize.

Nipple Ah but yoo're supposed t' be the Leader.

Scrawdyke Well never mind. It doesn't matter. 'E probably thought we were playin' some kind of game, just playin' around. Let's get on. Allard's unconscious on the bed. We 'ave the paintin' facin' 'im for when 'e comes round. (*He places an old canvas on an easel in the required position.*) An' we all stand ready. Me in the middle. Irwin there, Wick'll be there, an' Nipple there.

Nipple Are we just goin' t' wait for 'im t' come round? It could tek hours.

Scrawdyke No. Irwin 'll chuck some water over 'is 'ead.

Ingham Oh, what –

Scrawdyke In that jug.

Ingham Oh it's full.

Wick Ey, 'e's not goin' to –

Scrawdyke No just reckon, Irwin, just reckon.

Ingham makes a vague gesture with the jug in Wick's direction.

Now back in position. Our sticks.

He collects the sticks. Ingham puts down the jug. They resume position. The three of them stand there, masked, their sticks raised menacingly. Slowly Wick begins to move and groan, then he very dazedly raises his head a little, wipes his hand across his eyes, then peers at the three. When at last he seems to have got them into focus, Scrawdyke says:

Good evening, Mr Allard!

Nipple I'm going t' t' bog. (*Nipple goes out.*)

Scrawdyke Why did you seduce Margaret Thwaite?

Wick Margaret Thwaite?

Scrawdyke Please don't weary us by denying it.

Wick 'E's beginning to regain consciousness. 'Is cunnin' little brain's beginnin' t' work.

Scrawdyke We must expect it. After the first shock. We mustn't underestimate 'im.

Wick What proof have you?

Scrawdyke Ah so you admit there is something to be proved.

Wick I didn't say that.

Scrawdyke That's what you implied.

Wick Look here, Scrawdyke, what are your terms of reference?

Scrawdyke My eyes. The eyes of my comrades. The testimony of the girl herself.

Wick Now look here, Scrawdyke, suppose I admit that.

Scrawdyke Suppose nothing. I deal in facts. And if those aren't enough for you I need only mention –

Wick What?

Scrawdyke Eric Tomlinson.

Wick's mouth falls open, his eyes roll, he gasps for air.

Water!

Ingham In 'is face?

Scrawdyke To drink.

Ingham runs to sink, brings cup to Wick who seizes it, gulps down the water, then lies on his back panting.

Wick Ah, ah, ah, ah, ah, – but 'ow – 'ow, oh no, ah, ah –

Scrawdyke But surely, Mr Allard, you must 'ave suspected all along that I knew?

Wick Oh, oh, ah, ah, my – oh, ah, oh –

Slowly Wick sits up and brings himself to speak.

All right, Scrawdyke – I admit there is something in what you say – you're perfectly correct in your assumption that I did suspect you knew – but I could never be sure, and as time went on I began to imagine – I see now that I committed a major blunder in dismissing you. Yes you've got me. I seriously underestimated you. You've proved more than a match for me. God you're clever.

52

Scrawdyke I'll grant you that. That's one point on which we agree.

Wick Listen, Scrawdyke, I'm a reasonable man, let bygones be bygones, you can all return to the school.

Scrawdyke ostentatiously turns away, yawns.

I'll get you better grants!

Scrawdyke The British Centipedes fall into three orders. Those having fifteen body-segments, those having twenty-two body-segments, and those having thirty-one to 173 body-segments. Did you know that, Irwin?

Ingham Er – no.

Wick I'll make sure you all get NDD!

Scrawdyke It's a fact.

Wick I can do it, I have influence, I can pull strings!

Scrawdyke walks about humming to himself.

I'll get you into the Slade, Royal College, Rome Scholarship.

Scrawdyke looks out of the window, his back to Wick.

I'll appoint you deputy headmaster. I can fix it with higher authority. I have money, you can have it. My daughter, she's lovely, she's ripe, I –

Scrawdyke suddenly turns.

Scrawdyke I don't want your daughter! I don't want your money! I don't want your jobs! I don't want your scholarships!

Wick Then what do you want?

Scrawdyke I want you! (*Pause.*)

Wick What –

Scrawdyke I want you, in my power, utterly and completely! I want you to surrender every last vestige of self-respect to me. I want you to throw your worthless life on my mercy. I want you to give yourself completely into my keeping. I want to 'ollow you out and fill you in with nothing but 'umiliation. I want you to destroy yourself as a man in front of me. 'Ere. Now. In this room. Then I want t' see you crawl away an' cringe out the rest of y'r days in my shadow. I want you to become my excreta.

Wick sits stunned. Then suddenly, like a wild animal, he leaps up and hurls himself at the door. He pulls at it frantically, then, finding it won't open, he starts to pound on it frenziedly. Scrawdyke looks on unmoving, unsmiling. Ingham watches alarmed. As Wick's strength ebbs he sinks towards the floor, his blows get weaker. Finally he is a whimpering heap on the floor.

Pull y'self together, man. I expected better of you.

Scrawdyke gestures to Ingham to drag Wick over and prop him against the radio cabinet. Ingham does this. Wick is completely unresistant, an inert mass.

Listen! Are y' listenin'?

Wick whimpers weakly.

Wick Yeaas.

Scrawdyke You see this painting? (*He moves easel to central position.*) D' y' know what it is? I'll tell you what it is. It's one of the world's greatest masterpieces. *Garden at Cookham Rise* by Stanley Spencer.

Wick But –

Scrawdyke Never mind how we got it. It's 'ere, we're 'ere, an' so are you. That's all that matters. Full cast and props for the drama t' be enacted. It's very simple. In return for your smashing this painting we give you our silence. In return for your integrity we give you back your career.

Wick But, but – how do I know –

Scrawdyke 'Ow d' y' know we won't split on you after all? Y' don't. Y'll just 'ave t' trust us. An emotion you're not very familiar with. But y'll 'ave to try it. Just a little simple 'uman trust, Philip. We aren't all as black as you. Just put your trust in us, relax, let y'self go, have faith. For the first time in your life 'ave a little faith.

Wick I have no alternative. And – and I think you're a man of your word.

Scrawdyke Good. 'Elp Mr Allard to 'is feet, Irwin.

Ingham Oh – yeh.

Ingham helps Wick up. Wick stands tottering before the painting. Scrawdyke gets a hammer, he holds it out to Wick, who hesitates then takes it. Wick raises it and stands swaying in front of the painting. Pause. Then suddenly he smashes savagely at the canvas, ripping into it. His attack grows more furious with every blow. Scrawdyke eggs him on and Ingham starts to grin maliciously. Scrawdyke starts to chant, then Ingham joins in.

Scrawdyke Smash it! Smash it! Smash it! Smash it! Smash it! Smash it . . .

Ingham Smash it! Yes. Smash it! Smash it –

Wick hurls the painting from the easel and hits, tramples, snaps and tears at it on the floor until finally he is kicking and stamping on a twisted wreck. He comes to a standstill, exhausted. The chanting dies. They all stand motionless staring at the wreck. Then

Scrawdyke goes over to Wick, bends close to his ear, and whispers.

Scrawdyke Your trust was misplaced.

Wick looks up.

Now we 'ave ev'rything. Integrity and career.

Blackout

SCENE 4

Later the same afternoon. It is somewhat darker, as the scene
proceeds the daylight fades, going through the grey-blue of
snowy winter dusk until, by the last part of the scene, it is
dark outside and Scrawdyke and Wick are talking in almost
complete darkness, there only being the last vestiges of light
coming in through the window. Ingham is painting the
banner – Scrawdyke and Wick are sitting. Nipple enters.

Wick Aha 'ere it is.

Scrawdyke Y've been t' the gallery?

Nipple Mm.

Wick Y've checked up on the size of the paintin's?

Nipple Let me tell y'.

Scrawdyke All right give us y'r report.

Nipple Ai left where Ai live in Spaines Road an' boarded
a trolley, Ai knew that what was normally a short prosaic
journey was t' be mutated by the magic wand of winter
into an odyssey through the 'aunted chasms of perpetual
day – night. Ai 'ave a very strong sense of these things.
Through the wintry ghostlight of the snow the machine
wove sluggishly its pre-ordained way along the destiny
written with wire for it in the sky above. Seemin'ly
completely in its power, as if Ai and not it, were the
prisoner, Ai 'uddled shoulder t' shoulder with mai fellow-
travellers, inert as if 'ibernatin', givin' out nothing, yet
quick an' alive mai sense of mission lurked passionately
within the depths of mai skull. Aaaah –

57

Well, we got as far as that church, y' know, at t' bottom o' Wheat'ouse Road, an' a car 'ad skidded madly across the road in front of us, blockin' the way. The machine churned wearily to a standstill. Ai wrenched maiself from its shelter an' began to trudge through the snows of an 'Uddersfield-made Siberia. Men moved like Eskimos about me, an' Ai could feel as Ai –

Scrawdyke So you walked to the gallery. Did y' get the measurements?

Nipple Wait until A tell y'.

Scrawdyke We 'av'n't time. The putsch is scheduled for next Friday not 1969.

Wick We asked y' for a report not a fifteen-volume prose poem.

Nipple Waah –

Scrawdyke Did y' get the measurements?

Nipple Yes.

Wick Give 'em 'ere.

   Nipple gets a crumpled bit of paper out of his pocket.

Ta.

Scrawdyke Did y' check up on 'ow the paintin's are 'ung?

Nipple Yes. It's 'ow we said.

Wick Any of 'em'll go in that portfolio.

Scrawdyke Good.

Wick Let's 'ave some tea. (*Wick fills kettle, lights gas, puts kettle on, puts tea in pot, etc.*)

Nipple On me way 'ere from t' gallery Ai saw somebody yoo know.

Scrawdyke 'Oo?

Nipple One o' t' girls from t' Art School.

Scrawdyke That could be any one o' fifty.

Nipple Noe, noe, this's a partic'lar one. One yoo fancy.

Scrawdyke What d' y' mean I fancy?

Nipple Y' know which one Ai mean, what's 'er name? Ann. Ann something –

Wick Graves, Finley?

Nipple Noe.

Wick Ann Spencer, Anne Daniels –

Nipple No it's not that.

Wick Ann Gedge. Anne Waddington. Anne –

Nipple That's it, y' just –

Scrawdyke I never fancied Anne Waddington!

Nipple No, not 'er, the one y' said before.

Wick Gedge?

Nipple Yes that's the one.

Wick A never knew y' 'ad a yen for 'er, Mal.

Scrawdyke I didn't. 'E's in another of 'is fantasies.

Nipple Oh but y' do, y' told me, y' went on about the nape of 'er neck.

Wick Haha, a nape fetishist.

Scrawdyke I never said anything about the nape of 'er neck.

Nipple Oh y' did. Y' went on and on about it. About its slope an' the little groove in it.

Scrawdyke I never said anything . . . I don't go round lookin' for grooves in girls' necks. That's one of your perversions. I may 'ave made some general remark about 'er, she's not a bad-lookin' lass from what I remember. Though A'm not sure I'm thinkin' about the one you're talkin' about. There are so many birds down in that place, they're all alike.

Nipple Noe –

Wick I know 'er, I 'ad a session with 'er once. Durin' that dance we 'ad last year she got me t' tek 'er outside an' – Well, a right little virgin she turned out t' be. Y' know scared stiff. Yeh she's a – Anyway A just got browned off.

Nipple Ai c'n always tell when a woman's ready to go. It's a matter of intuition. A mysterious chemical combination drawin' y' together.

Wick Is that so.

Nipple Women respond t' me, they sense – something in me. Ai wish Ai 'ad a shillin' for all the girls Ai've been out with. Ai seem t' attract ev'ry sort from shy little shop assistants t' darin' intellectual women. Ai 'ave this certain inner magnet which pulls 'em towards me. They sense the pristine animal in me, hee hee. It's ev'ry age group as well. Even married women with kids are drawn towards mee. Their reason tries t' struggle but it's futile, they finally abandon themselves an' lose themselves – Sometimes Ai try t' restrain meself, knowin' the 'avoc Ai'll wreak in these women's lives. But it's no use, Ai 'ave t' give in t' the ineluctable – suckin' force within me. The 'ole fabric of these women's lives is cast away for one savage moment of ecstasy. One woman can't satisfy me for long an' Ai 'ave t' move on. Ai just can't 'elp meself – There was this woman at this party. She was the wife of some jazz musician 'oo'd come over from Leeds. She 'ad Negro blood in 'er, y' know, y' could tell. She 'ad this dark pigmented skin and these untamed eyes, these sensual thick fleshy lips. She 'ad these 'eavy heavin' breasts, a narrer waist, an' great rounded fecund 'ips that she swung provocatively ev'ry time she moved. She 'ad this taut dress on an' nothing underneath – Ai found that out later. It was as tight as a drum-skin an' y' could see ev'ry sensual tremor in 'er body. She moved with this rhythm like a black she-panther. Aaaaah – Well when Ai got there she was by 'erself like at one side. She seemed t' be detached from it all, bored and caged in by all the pale in'ibited males from this area 'oo surrounded 'er. Then she saw me! An' there was this immediate recognition, this sexual spark flashed between us! Our eyes mated. She was transformed – Well, A thought, Ai'll let things take their natural course. Ai'll let 'er come to me. Ai won't make it too easy for 'er, Ai'll let 'er 'unt me down. So Ai got a drink an' chatted t' people over the other side of the room. Not lookin' at 'er but sensin' all the time 'er presence, comin' nearer, bein' drawn ineluctably. Sure enough Ai turn an' there she is, sort of tremblin' by me side. We didn't speak. There was no need for mundane words. Before we knew it we were clasped together pulsatin'. Pulsatin' t' the music in a crazy primordial frenzy. Our mouths gnawed 'ungrily at each other. 'Er thick fleshy 'ot lips engulfed me. Our tongues conversed with a wet, wanton wildness, writhin' an' twistin' like angry snakes. She suddenly bit into me tongue, sinkin' 'er teeth in, the spasm of pain shot through me. But it wasn't a pain like an ordinary pain. It was an ecstatic flame 'at lept through mai innards makin' 'em throb an' glow. Before Ai knew it we were upstairs in a bedroom. An' she – she'd unzipped me! An' she 'ad mai – she 'ad it in 'er 'and! An' she was squeezin'. An' she said: 'Do anything to me. 'Urt me. Tear me. Tear me. Make me feel.' An' I sez, Ai sez, Ai sez: 'What d' y' want me t' do?' An' she starts rippin' at me, tearin' me clo'es off, clawin'

off me shirt, wrenchin' off me pants. An' Ai'm tearing off
'er frock, an' we fall, tearin' on the bed. An' we fuse
together in t' one white 'ot furnace of fusion – An' Ai c'n
'ear the toms toms of 'er ancestors drummin' in me ears, in
me blood, in me thighs – An' ev'rything's obliterated.
'Uddersfield dissolves, Yorkshire disappears. The twentieth
century – the's only this moment, this act of pure savage
elemental being. There in that room. Just this furnace. Just
this energy. Just this – (*Pause.*)

Wick Just one question.

Nipple Ai never saw 'er again.

Wick What was the record y' danced to?

Nipple What a woman! She was a woman 'at even Ai
could 'ave gone with more than once.

Wick Bit 'eavy on clothes though.

Nipple 'Oo cares about shirts.

Wick Very true. Next time she comes over let me know.
A've got a couple of old shirts she's quite welcome t' rip off
me. D' y' think A should wear two shirts t' prolong the
ecstasy?

> *The water should be boiling about here. Wick makes the
> tea. During the following conversation they all get
> themselves some.*

Well Irwin, 'ow did y' like the sound o' that then.

Ingham Oh well – aye – it sounded – int'restin'.

Wick Y' see y've got 'im int'rested. Y' shouldn't go tellin'
stories like that in front of Irwin 'ere. 'E won't 'ave any
time for 'is raffia work now. 'E'll be runnin' round
'Uddersfield lookin' for Negro women wi' drum-tight
skirts an' untamed eyes. 'E won't rest until 'e's 'eard them

tom toms. The's goin' to be a nasty incident on a corporation trolley. Y'd better walk 'ome from now on Irwin. We don't want war wi' Jamaica.

Nipple Hee hee.

Scrawdyke There's just one thing y' forgot t' mention.

Nipple What?

Scrawdyke I was at that party.

Nipple Y' weren't.

Scrawdyke I was. It was up at 'Arry Sutton's.

Wick Ey, y' saw this primordial sex goddess?

Scrawdyke I saw 'er. A pale, skinny little kid with a spotty face an' a slight squint. 'Er eyes were untamed all right, she couldn't focus 'em. An' as for a drum-tight skirt, if y'd made a frock for 'er out of an 'andkerchief, it'd 'ave 'ung like a tent. If she didn't wear underwear it was because she didn't need to. 'Er chances of bein' bothered were less than nil until this pristine animal arrived on t' scene. Y' know, she was the only bird left, an' even then, desperate as she was, it was an 'ard job for the Memoirs of Casanova t' make 'er. Even though she was a beggar she was still a bit choosy.

Nipple You weren't there.

Wick So it was all a big fib, Nipple.

Nipple Waargh. Ai'm goin' for a pee.

Wick Tell us all about it when y' come back. I'm in the mood for a good adventure story.

Nipple goes out. We hear feet plodding upstairs.

What a deluded –!

Scrawdyke Yeh. Let's 'ave some more tea.

He gets himself some tea. Wick goes and looks at Ingham.

Wick 'Ow's it goin'?

Ingham Oh – A've nearly finished.

Wick Yeh. It's great. It'll look good unfurled above us as we march. The symbol of Dynamic Erection.

Scrawdyke Aye.

Footsteps. Nipple comes in.

Nipple Ai'm off now. Ai want t' get on with some work.

Scrawdyke Well shut the bloody door it's freezin'.

Wick Ah, y're goin' off t' slave over an 'ot page. To add a few more tellin' paragraphs to the Novel of the Twentieth Century.

Nipple Mm.

Wick 'Ow far've y' got with it now?

Nipple Well Ai'm still werkin' on the first movement.

Wick 'Ow many chapters?

Nipple It doesn't 'ave chapters. It just 'as these movements.

Wick T' first movement plods, t' second movement stands still, and t' third movement drops dead.

Nipple 'Ow would yoo know, y've not read it.

Wick No but I've 'eard you talk about it. Indeed I'll go further, I've 'eard you talk it.

Nipple Waah.

Wick Tell me, is the rumour true that you and your novel are one and the same? Or are you just good friends?

Nipple What d' y' –?

Wick Y've been talkin' this novel ever since A met y'. You're a case of a man written by a book.

Nipple Err, very funny. Just becos Ai 'ave a gift for verbal –

Wick That stuff about the Negress, A bet that's goin' in.

Nipple Maybee.

Wick Am I goin' in?

Nipple Noe.

Wick But I'm a very int'restin' character.

Nipple Ai don't deel in characters.

Wick Well what do y' deal in?

Nipple The quest. The quest for the reel be'ind the tawdry panoply of seemin' –

Wick A Western?

Nipple Ai like t' think of it as a metaphysical strip show.

Wick That sounds a bit near the knuckle. It doesn't sound like the kind of book I'd let my maid read.

Nipple It won't be an easy werk t' grasp. Ai make demands.

Wick What's it called?

Nipple *From out the Cocoon.*

Wick Portrait of the Artist As a Young Bug.

Nipple Ah well Ai'm not goin' t' bandy words. It's unworthy of me. When's the next meetin'?

Scrawdyke Tomorra afternoon.

Nipple What time?

Scrawdyke About two.

Wick Scrawdyke the fourth tomorra.

Nipple Well A'll see y'.

Wick S'long.

Ingham Aye, s'long. (*He goes.*)

Wick What a nutter!

Scrawdyke 'E's not a person 'e's an absurdity.

Wick 'E's never 'ad owt published?

Scrawdyke 'As 'e 'eck. 'E lives on National Assistance.

Ingham Well A've finished this now, like, Mal. It just needs t' dry, like.

Wick Y've done a bloody good job, Irwin.

Scrawdyke It'll do.

Ingham Aye, well A think A'd better be off an' all now. That is unless o' course –

Wick Ah y've got an assignation wi' one o' these Negresses 'ave y'?

Ingham Nay A wish A 'ad.

Wick Just one o' these pale-pelted 'Uddersfield beauties is it? Wi' breasts n' bigger'n bee stings.

Ingham No it's just me tea.

Wick 'Ow y' goin' t' 'andle y' mam?

Ingham Well like A'll 'ave t' some'ow make 'er think like 'at, well, 'at A'm considerin' goin' back – A mean not 'at I

66

er – but anyway. Until A move in 'ere. Ooh it's not goin' t' be easy. A'm not lookin' forward to it.

Scrawdyke Just do it.

Ingham Aye. Well A'm off then.

Scrawdyke OK.

Ingham Oh – er – like, Mal.

Wick A thought y'd decided t' go?

Ingham I 'ave but – Well A was goin' t' say – A mean what A was goin' t' say was well A thought like – A mean unless you 'ave some other – Well, anyway A thought like A might well, pop, y' know just pop, up t' t' Jazz Club for an hour or so t'night. Y' know if the's nothing 'at –

Scrawdyke It costs two bob t' get in t' that Jazz Club. We need ev'ry penny we've for got the struggle. We can't squander.

Ingham Aye A know, Mal. But A thought like A might be able t' get in for nowt. Y' know if the's somebody 'oo knows me like on t' door.

Scrawdyke Nah. I know you. If they ask y' t' pay, y' will.

Ingham Oh all right a'm off.

Scrawdyke Don't go near that Jazz Club.

Ingham Right. S'long. (*Ingham goes.*)

Wick A wu'n't mind goin' up t' that Jazz Club meself.

Scrawdyke Aye, well we will.

Wick Aha.

Scrawdyke I can always get in for nothing. In fact they usually refuse t' take my money even if I offer it. I know 'em all, Keith Smith, Archy, Trevor Kaye, Selwyn, Mike

Clay. I introduced most of 'em t' Jazz in t' first place. I was probably the first person in this town to understand what Jazz is.

Wick Oh aye they all know me an' all. You an' me an' one or two others are jazz in this town.

Scrawdyke Yeh.

Wick A wonder when Selwyn's goin' t' come for that drum?

Scrawdyke D'know. It's been 'ere three weeks.

Wick Aye, well 'e's usin' that other.

Scrawdyke That one he –

Wick Yeh.

Scrawdyke Anyway we'll go. It'll be a shrewd move. If we appear there just as usual nobody'll suspect owt.

Wick Aye we must be'ave as if nothin's 'appenin'. If we don't go they'll start –

Scrawdyke We've got to go.

Wick We can't avoid it. (*Pause.*) Well it's not snowin' at the moment. Foo but it's cold. Seems t' be gettin' colder. That stupid little thing's been on all day an' it's still freezin'. Ha but we're goin' t'warm things up next Friday!

Scrawdyke Aye. Put that Gerry Mulligan on.

Wick Yes that's just what we need. (*Wick puts on 'Frenesi' by the original Gerry Mulligan Quartet.*)

Scrawdyke This's just the weather for our conspiracy. Y' need extreme weather as a background to extreme action. It 'eightens it. Gives it an epic quality. Great 'eat or great cold. That's what y' need.

Wick Mild days are for mild men. The average temperature's for the average man.

Scrawdyke Yeh.

Wick It was snowin' in Petrograd.

Scrawdyke Mussolini marched on Rome in an 'eat wave.

Wick It was blazin' in Sarajevo when Princip let 'im 'ave it.

Scrawdyke January 1933 was the coldest January for fifteen years.

Wick Was it?

Scrawdyke Yes.

Wick A wonder if it was as cold as this?

Scrawdyke It wasn't.

Wick That's a good omen. Friday, Scrawdyke the ninth, Year One. It's goin' t' be our October Revolution, our Easter Week, our July twentieth, our Burning of the Reichstag, our –

Scrawdyke Our Conquest of Mexico.

Wick A say, Mal, between you an' me, when we get t' power, what are goin' t' be our aims, A mean our real aims? What a' we goin' t' do with it?

Scrawdyke Between ourselves?

Wick Yeh.

Scrawdyke Nothing!

Wick Nothing?

Scrawdyke We want power purely for its own sake.

Wick To enjoy it.

Scrawdyke We shan't pursue any specific policy for its intrinsic value.

Wick What we do with it doesn't matter.

Scrawdyke In that sense we shall do nothing.

Wick But there'll be plenty activity.

Scrawdyke Purely arbitrary activity.

Wick Perverse activity.

Scrawdyke Strictly for giggles.

Wick Our giggles.

Scrawdyke The Absurd State.

Wick Absurdity with vengeance.

Scrawdyke Naked unadorned vengeance. Ten thousand years of culture will be given into our hands, for our safe-keeping, and we will let it fall, shattering it completely.

Wick And the Bomb?

Scrawdyke Drop it.

Wick Of course.

Scrawdyke Cruelty.

Wick For its own sake.

Scrawdyke No excuses. Our whim, that will be morality.

Wick The freedom of the one demands the servitude of the many.

Scrawdyke Which is what they really desire.

Wick Which is what they crave.

Scrawdyke We shall rear up our soaring pyramids dedicated to nothing. The millions will climb the steps in pain to vanish at the top. Agony will be the order of our new day. If you ask me for Justice I will punch you in the mouth. If you ask me for Mercy I will kick you in the balls! If you ask me for Love I will knock you to the ground. And if you ask me for Truth I will show you my fist, my boot and my laughing face!

Wick (*quietly*) The Final Solution of the Human Question.

Music stops.

Blackout

SCENE 5

*The boom, boom, boom, of a drum. Lights up. It is dark
outside. The four are marching round the room in a tight
formation. Scrawdyke is slightly ahead, by his side Wick
carries the banner. Behind them march Ingham, banging
the drum, and Nipple. All except Ingham have their arms
raised in the party salute. They go round the room once,
twice. Nipple begins to lag behind a tiny bit. They go
round a third time.*

Wick We arrive at the Market Cross.

*They line up in front of the table. Ingham changes
rhythm to a slower beat. Wick runs to tape recorder and
switches on an anthem. Then he resumes his position in
the line. Scrawdyke walks gravely down the line,
inspecting and shaking hands with each one in turn,
starting off with a couple of phantom members. When
he gets to Nipple he adjusts his duffle coat as if it is a
uniform slightly out of order.*

Nipple Waa –

*Scrawdyke mounts the table by means of the radio
cabinet. Wick moves to the tape recorder and switches it
on. Scrawdyke stands saluting. Mass crowd cheers
resound from the recorder. Wick fades them off and
mounts the radio cabinet which is just by him.*

Wick Malcolm Scrawdyke. On behalf of the Party, on
behalf of the Nation, I address you. At this critical
moment in world history I call upon you. You, and you
alone, are our saviour. You are the Supreme Embodiment

of all that is finest in Human Nature. You are the finest flowering of Mankind. You are the fount of our wisdom, you are the source of our strength, you are our Bastion against Eunarchy. You are our hope, guide and example for the next three thousand years. Dynamic Erection is the Future! Malcolm Scrawdyke is Dynamic Erection! Malcolm Scrawdyke is the Future!

Switches tape on. Loud chanting – Hail Scrawdyke, Hail Scrawdyke, Hail Scrawdyke – recorded over and over again by the four to produce the effect of a vast number. Scrawdyke waits, then gives a small wave meaning silence. Wick turns knob. Chanting is faded out.

Scrawdyke Friends. Fellow fighters. People of the Nation.

Two years ago I woke from the troubled sleep of apathy. There was borne upon me a dreadful feeling that something was wrong with the state of our country. Seeking the cause of this dismal intuition, I looked around me. On every side I saw decadence, cynicism, apathy and decay. For seventeen months, try as I might, by night or by day, I could not rid myself of the spectre that haunted me. In bed, on the street, at work and at play it was always before me. The spectre of a dying culture, materially fat but completely lacking in any of the spiritual direction, promise and aspiration which made our race great over the millennia.

At first, I was bewildered, I was completely unable to grasp the situation. How can this be? I asked myself. How could it happen? Where are the leaders, mentors, and poets who throughout History have been the guardians against such catastrophe? I sought the giants who would carry me on their broad backs out of the darkness. I sought in vain. Such mythical creatures are nowhere to be found. They no longer exist. We must become the giants ourselves!

*Roar of approval from tape recorder. As it fades
Scrawdyke continues.*

Hemmed in on every side, pressed to our last gasp by the
massed hordes of militant Eunarchy, those who are
castrated themselves and whose sole aim is to castrate us
to their level, surrounded by these eunuchs I realized that
we the oppressed must take matters into our own hands.
We must rally our forces and seize the initiative.

Another roar. As it subsides:

I am fighting for a new clean day, when young people can
stand upright in dignity, when no one need be afraid of
their next thought, when frankness and honesty are
universally respected, when power in the State is drawn
from virtue. I call upon you all to follow the Party of
Dynamic Erection which has already so decisively lit a
blazing beacon here in Huddersfield that makes men shield
their eyes across the continents.

Roar grows towards end of speech.

I say join us now and sweep to the power which is your
birthright. Once and for all time let us obliterate the scum
from the face of the earth. Give me your present and I will
give you the Future. I am Scrawdyke and I am here! I
promise, I pledge, I promise, I will, I offer you one thing
and one thing alone, I offer you Dignity!

*Sustained roar. After a while it changes to the chant:
Hail Scrawdyke, Hail Scrawdyke, Hail Scrawdyke, Hail
Scrawdyke –
Scrawdyke steps down from the table.*

Wick The crowd's surgin' round y'.

Scrawdyke Yeh. They're frenzied with approval. (*He nods
and acknowledges crowd.*)

Wick Come on, Irwin, it's your duty t' protect the Leader.

Ingham Eh?

Wick Keep close to 'im.

Nipple Look out the's an assissin.

Scrawdyke Where?

Nipple 'Ere.

Wick OK y're comin' at 'im.

Nipple 'E doesn't see me.

Scrawdyke I do.

Wick Y've got a knife.

Nipple A gun.

Scrawdyke Both!

Nipple Ai'm goin' t' use – noe Ai won't tell y'.

Wick Irwin, the ever-alert bodyguard spots 'im. Not me, Irwin. 'Im – Come on do y' stuff, man!

Ingham What?

Wick 'Url y'self between the Leader an' 'is assailant.

Ingham There isn't room.

Scrawdyke Get back, Nipple. Don't be so bloody impetuous.

Wick takes the banner and props it up at the back on the room so that it forms a background.

Nipple Waah, Ai could 'ave killed y' five times by this –

Wick Get back. Right. Now start again.

Nipple Ai'm smilin' as if Ai'm goin' t' shake 'ands with the great man.

Wick But Irwin isn't fooled! Go on.

Pushes Ingham who falls awkwardly between Nipple and Scrawdyke and half-heartedly pushes at Nipple.

Scrawdyke Go on, Irwin, tackle 'im.

Nipple Noe, noe, y' don't manage –

Wick Course 'e does, y're not suggestin' y' succeed, are y'?

Nipple Hee hee.

Scrawdyke Aye that's a role you'd like, i'n't it?

Nipple Well, y' ought t' be grateful. 'Oo else'd go t' trouble t' kill yoo?

Scrawdyke I 'ave many enemies. I 'ave the capacity to arouse deep antagonisms.

Nipple Noe. Ai'd say in the main most people liked y'.

Scrawdyke How ridiculous can y' get?

Wick Come on get on wi' this attempted assassination. Irwin pushes you off an' grabs the knife.

Nipple Noe, not yet, Ai –

He gives Ingham a clumsy but powerful shove. Ingham is annoyed. Ingham rushes at Nipple with surprising ferocity. He pushes and pummels Nipple for a moment until his sudden spurt of anger abates.

Ey give up. Ey stop. Noe. Ugh. That 'urt. Noe stop it –

Wick switches the tape recorder off.

Scrawdyke OK, lads that's it. Irwin y've successfully saved my life.

Wick An' you're dead.

Nipple Noe, noe, Ai've escaped.

Wick 'Ow could y' possibly 'ave escaped? Irwin 'ad 'old of y'.

Nipple Err, 'e took it too seriously but Ai –

Ingham A'm sorry like if A –, but –

Nipple Noe, Ai mean 'e wouldn't 'ave 'ad a chance t' do all that if it was reel. Ai'd just fire at point blank range an' then in the confusion Ai'd just run –

Wick You can't run.

Nipple 'Course Ai c'n run.

Wick All right, actions speak louder 'an words. Let's see y'!

Nipple Waagh. Don't be –

Wick Let's see y'.

Nipple Waar – Ai can't in 'ere, it's too small.

Wick runs round the room very rapidly.

Aar well –

Wick Your turn!

Nipple Ai could if Ai –

Wick It's all yours.

Nipple Waar – (*Pause. Nipple starts to lumber.*)

Wick Aha. As A said y're dead.

Blackout

SCENE 6

Lights up. Dark outside. Scrawdyke is pacing about.

Scrawdyke Monday morning. Monday morning already. I've got to have another go at Ann tonight. Oh it's got t' be better than last Friday's 'eroic performance. Got down to 'er place, didn't even manage t' get through t' garden gate. If I 'adn't bumped into 'er as I scuttled away I wouldn't 'ave even seen 'er. Told 'er all about the Party, worked meself into a frenzy. And what did she say? 'Sounds difficult.' That was it. That was 'er reaction. That's the tremendous impact I made! Now come on. It's no use cryin' over spilled – Scrawdyke. I've got to work this out. Now – well she 'as t' walk up Princess Street. That's 'er quickest way t' trolley stop in front o' t' Co-op. Suppose she comes – There's only one other way she can get there, on Buxton Road. Yes, I know, I can 'ide in that tunnel by Whitfield's shop. One end looks down on Princess Street t' other end comes out on Buxton Road. So I'm in the tunnel. (*He acts this out.*) So I watch down – Then I run up t' t' other end. I keep a constant watch. One way – then t' other. I see 'er comin' – say up Princess Street, that's most likely. I watch 'er walk up. She might see me! No, no, it's dark. Lurk, man, lurk. Right, I watch 'er. She comes up past. Suppose she's got somebody wi' 'er. Oh they'll leave 'er at t' top. I run up t' other end an' I can see 'er go t' t' stop. What if a trolley comes and picks 'er up before I can get there? Oh well, that can't be 'elped. It's unlikely, unlikely, unlikely. So I see 'er – then I come out. Walk on towards 'er casual, just walkin', upright, dignified. An' when I get by 'er, I just see 'er, by accident. What if I falter?

78

I won't. I see 'er – 'Ah, hullo. Just come up from Tech? I'm just on me way back to the Studio. Been out for a bit of a stroll y' know. Look why don't y' pop in for a cup o' tea if y're not doin' anything. You invited me down t' your place an' I'd like t' return the compliment. It's not exactly a pent'ouse but it 'as one or two amusin' features.'

Get 'er in 'ere. Sit 'er down. Fire. Tea. Record. Then – Tell 'er. Yes. Explain. I need 'er. I want 'er. I'm shy – Oh I c'n do it. The right atmosphere. I'm a remarkable man. She'll soon see that. Once she understands, I'm away. The's not really anything t' stop me. The 'ole thing's organic. I shall triumph.

'I'm glad I bumped into you Ann because there are one or two things I'd like to say to you. To begin with I must make it clear that I am afflicted by shyness. And like all who suffer this affliction my behaviour is often misconstrued. I –

Blackout

79

SCENE 7

Wick Monday, Scrawdyke the fifth, Year One.

Scrawdyke Only three days t' go before the Great Day begins.

Wick The beginning of the New Era.

Ingham comes in, carrying a bundled sleeping-bag under his arm.

'Ail Scrawdyke.

Ingham 'Ail Scrawdyke. A've brought me sleepin'-bag. Oooh it's cold.

Wick Aye there are six-foot drifts up our way.

Ingham Listen, like, A've got summat t' tell y'.

Scrawdyke What?

Ingham Well, A were just gettin' off t' trolley – they're still runnin' all right but they're a bit – well anyway A just got off y' know, where it stops just outside t' Pack'orse front –

Scrawdyke Yeh, yeh.

Ingham Ay well. A just got off an' A bumped int' Eric Boocock –

Scrawdyke I 'ope y' didn't damage 'im. I want 'im 'ole for 'is trial.

Wick Yeh 'e's on our list.

Ingham Aye, well, anyway 'e's walkin' up, y' know on 'is way back t' Tech, so like A walked on Cross Church Street with 'im, well some o' t' way, A left 'im by Jackson's. Anyway, 'e sez, like, there was this meetin' this mornin' an' Allard told 'em about – It appears like 'at Allard, this mornin' called 'em all in t' t' end room at eleven o'clock. An' 'e tells 'em 'ow me an' John 'ave – well, left like. 'Ow we'd – A mean this's the way 'e put it – 'ow we'd gone against 'im. An' then, apparently, A mean so Eric said, 'e tells 'em like as 'ow we've all 'ad it now – A mean from what – well, could be called a careers – y' know. An' 'ow it's a – it's a – Well that doesn't – Anyway – that's what 'er –

Scrawdyke 'An' 'ow it's' what?

Ingham Eh?

Scrawdyke Y' started t' say summat then y' –

Ingham Oh well that was – er – A mean it wasn't anything.

Scrawdyke I'm orderin' y' t' tell me what it is.

Ingham Oh, well, it was something an' nothin'. Just that, y' know, 'e just said 'e thought we were both, t' some extent – very promisin' – students – an' by leavin' we've spoilt – A mean this's just what 'e thinks. That's all. A mean the's nothing . . .

Pause. The information has made Wick thoughtful.

Scrawdyke Well, lads, y' can see what 'e's tryin' t' do. I must say I'm surprised 'at even 'e'd stoop t' such a feeble old trick.

Ingham What d' y' –?

Scrawdyke It stands out a mile, Irwin. Boocock wasn't at your bus stop by accident. 'E was planted there by Allard. 'E's just one of Allard's agents. 'E was deliberately sent there t' tell y' all this stuff about promisin' students t' try and make y' discontented. It's the oldest trick in the book.

81

Huh, 'ere I've been goin' on about not underestimatin' 'im. That'd be impossible. If this's the level on which 'is mind works – It's goin' t' be such a pushover we shan't even need t' be 'ere. It'll 'appen by itself. We can all leave town. Go out in t' t' fields an' make a snowman.

I'm disappointed, I was lookin' forward to some ex'ilaratin' action. Now I can see our only problem's goin' t' be stiflin' the yawns. (*Pause*.)

Wick Yeh, yeh –

Scrawdyke With every hour I grow more confident. With every minute our task seems easier. I 'ave no worries about Allard. If I 'ave any worries at all, they concern quite a diff'rent personage.

Ingham 'Oo?

Scrawdyke Isn't it obvious? Nipple.

Wick Y' mean 'e's not t' be trusted.

Scrawdyke That's exactly what I mean.

Wick 'E's plannin' to betray us.

Scrawdyke I'm afraid so.

Ingham But what makes y' think that?

Scrawdyke 'E's paranoid. 'E 'as all the usual symptoms.

Wick Aye.

Ingham 'Ow d' y' mean?

Scrawdyke Paranoea, clinically defined, is a syndrome comprising: delusions of grandeur, persecution mania, inability to reciprocate positive emotions, love, trust, etc., alienation from environment. All contributing to, and forming a part of, a general tendency to inhabit a world of fantasy.

Wick That's a perfect description of Nipple.

Scrawdyke 'E's bound to betray us. It's a compulsion with 'im.

Wick 'E'd betray us even if 'e didn't want to.

Ingham Then why did y' –?

Scrawdyke Why did I bring 'im in? Good question Irwin. I brought 'im in so that we could 'ave some control over 'im. Better to 'ave 'im plottin' on the inside than from the outside.

Wick That assassination business wasn't just a game to Nipple.

Scrawdyke It certainly wasn't. It revealed 'is true feelings. But we shall get in first. We must anticipate the event. We must conceive the exact nature of Nipple's treachery before 'e's 'ad a chance to conceive it for 'imself.

Wick Charge 'im with it before 'e's even thought of it.

Scrawdyke Such is the nature of political foresight.

Wick What 'as 'e done then?

Scrawdyke 'E's certainly 'ad a secret meetin' with Allard.

Wick Of course, where an' when?

Scrawdyke After dark.

Wick 'E sent a message to Allard.

Scrawdyke 'E did.

Wick 'E disguised 'imself as a crocodile an' unobtrusively made 'is way into the Art School where 'e lingered outside Allard's door. When Allard came out 'e bit 'im on the ankle and lower leg then swiftly made 'is getaway. When Allard came to examine the bite marks 'e discovered that they formed a message in cuneiform script.

Scrawdyke God, 'e's a cunning bastard.

Wick Unfortunately Nipple's spelling let 'im down an' Allard ended up treadin' water for three hours in the Public Baths at Cleck'eaton.

Scrawdyke 'E phoned Allard.

Wick An' where did they meet?

Scrawdyke Er – I know. At the top of St Paul's church tower!

Wick Yeh. Haha. Nobody'd think of goin' up there.

Scrawdyke Yeh. The's a little narrer ledge just at the base o' t' actual spire. Y' know it's just a little parapet thing about two feet wide.

Ingham Oh aye, we climbed up there last summer.

Wick Aye when we were doin' Arts Ball decorations in t' church.

Scrawdyke Y' go through a little door 'idden in t' foyer, at t' base o' t' tower.

Wick Yeh. Yeh the's just room t' squeeze y' way up them stairs an' they're so bloody steep. The's no light an' it's all coated wi' pigeon muck.

Scrawdyke The perfect settin'. Especially in this weather.

Ingham Oo I wou'n't like to 'ave t' go up there in this weather.

Scrawdyke It's just the place. It combines idiocy with infamy.

Wick Yeh. When did they meet there.

Scrawdyke Oh let's say they met there t'night. In a few hours' time. At six seventeen.

Wick Right. Let's make a tower.

Wick starts piling chairs and boxes on top of the table to form a spire. Scrawdyke helps him. They chuckle. Ingham is amused too.

Scrawdyke Good.

Wick We've got just the – (*He goes to the tape recorder and runs it until he gets loud howling wind.*) Remember this?

Scrawdyke Oh yeh. We used it for that –

Ingham Oh that.

Wick Aye A never wiped it off.

Scrawdyke Great. Now Nipple goes t' t' church first, 'e goes through that little door an' 'e starts t' grope up that spiral staircase.

Scrawdyke, as Nipple, starts climbing round and round and round on the same spot, laboriously, and ever more wearily.

'E's forgotten t' bring a torch.

Lights match and peering myopically continues. Match goes out. He gropes constrictedly.

Wick Allard arrives ten minutes later an' starts.

Wick starts spiralling.

'E 'asn't got a torch either. Too cautious. Doesn't want t' be seen.

Scrawdyke A pigeon craps on Nipple's 'ead. Daargh! Finally 'e nears the top. (*He drags himself the last few* *steps, each one a tremendous effort, the last step being on to the table by means of a chair. On the ledge he presses himself against the spire.*) It's freezin'. T' snow's teemin' down. It's pitch dark. T' wind nearly pulls 'im off t' ledge.

Wick God A'm getting dizzy.

Scrawdyke is edging his way round the spire.

Allard reaches the summit.

Wick gets on to the table and starts edging round the spire in the opposite direction to Scrawdyke. Moving crab-wise pressed flat against the spire they draw nearer and nearer to one another, until they bump, pressed shoulder to shoulder.

It is said that the rain in Spain falls mainly on the plain.

Scrawdyke Noe y've got it wrong. The's noe, 'It is said', yoo've put that in. Y' should 'ave just said, 'The rain in Spain falls mainly on the plain.'

Wick That is outside my terms of reference. I take it that you are the person with whom I have an appointment.

Scrawdyke Don't bee precipitate. Ai've got t' say mai part first.

Wick I realize that there is a certain protocol in these matters but I urge you to make haste.

Scrawdyke Say yours again.

Wick Oh very well, if you insist. The rain in Spain falls mainly on the plain.

Scrawdyke Except in July when none falls from the sky. Yoo're late!

Wick I apologize.

Scrawdyke Keep movin'. It's less suspicious.

They edge precariously round, frozen and unable to see, in danger of being torn from the ledge by the wind.

Wick I believe you have something to tell me.

Scrawdyke Scrawdyke is goin' to kidnap yoo on Friday night.

Wick What time?

Scrawdyke Nine o'clock.

Wick Good God! Are you certain of the validity of this statement?

Scrawdyke Certain.

Wick Then on the basis of this information I shall undertake certain measures.

Scrawdyke What about mai reward?

Wick I will ensure that you get the scholarship to study in Tahiti. You're sure no one knows of this meeting?

Scrawdyke stops. Wick goes on moving.

Where are you?

Scrawdyke Ai'm 'ere. Where are yoo?

Wick I'm here. Where have you gone?

Scrawdyke Ai'm here.

Wick Where?

Scrawdyke 'Ere.

Wick The other side?

Scrawdyke Come to mee.

Wick No you come to me.

Scrawdyke Noe, noe, yoo come to mee.

Wick No, no, you come to me.

Scrawdyke Noe you come to mee.

Wick All right stay where you are.

Scrawdyke Which way are yoo comin'?

Wick I don't know. I've lost all sense of direction.

Wick gropes round, and not seeing Scrawdyke is on top of him before he realizes it. They are squeezed on top of each other.

Aah!

Scrawdyke Get away. Get away.

Wick You move out of the way.

Scrawdyke Noe yoo move out of the way.

Wick Let me pass.

Scrawdyke Noe let me pass.

Wick Let me –

Scrawdyke ⎱ Let mee, let mee
Wick　　　⎰ Let me, let me –

They struggle, entangled together.

Wick I am the Principal of a School of Art.

Scrawdyke Ai am a great novelist.

They fall off –

Wick　　　 ⎱ Aaaaaaaaaaaaaaa –
Scrawdyke ⎰

– on to the floor where they roll about laughing then dog-hooting. Scrawdyke sits up.

Scrawdyke Well Irwin I 'ope you took note of all that because you are the witness.

Ingham Witness?

Wick Yes man. You saw it all

Ingham Well where am I supposed to 'ave been?

Wick Sittin' on the lightning conductor.

Scrawdyke Where were you Irwin at approximately six seventeen this evening?

Ingham On top o' St Paul's Church tower.

Blackout

SCENE 8

Scrawdyke comes in. Remains in the dark.

Scrawdyke Go back! Go back! Go back! No I – Oh I walked straight past. Straight past – I just couldn't make – Straight on. Did she see me? Oh I don't know. Didn't even dare look at 'er. Oh! – Go back now before – No, no. Oh let's face it! Let's face it this's the end of any – I've shown meself just now – completely spineless. I'm the most feeble. Ough! It makes me so – I want t' – Do something! Get! Hurt! Nipple! I'll get that bastard tomorrow. I've got t' get my – I'll show 'im! This's a bill that 'e can pay!

SCENE 9

Lights up. Afternoon light is fading. Scrawdyke, Wick and Ingham are sitting about. Nipple's tread on the stairs. They all watch the door. Nipple enters. Scrawdyke points at him.

Nipple What are yoo pointin' that finger at?

Scrawdyke Traitor!

Nipple Eh?

Scrawdyke Tergiversator!

Wick gets up, gestures to Ingham and they start removing the boxes from the table and arranging the room for a trial. Scrawdyke's chair behind the table, chairs for witness and prosecutor, tea chest for prisoner, banner propped up behind Scrawdyke's chair.

Wick OK. Nipple the game's up. The cat's out of the bag, the beans 'ave been spilled.

Nipple Err – Another of your elaborate jokes Ai suppose.

Scrawdyke It's no joke.

Wick I've never 'eard of anything so unfunny.

Nipple What the 'eck are y' talkin' about?

Scrawdyke I have just received incontestable proof that at six seventeen yesterday evening you met and conspired with Philip Allard, Arch Eunuch, and Enemy of the Party, at the top of St Paul's Church tower with the purpose of betraying the Dynamic Erectionist Movement.

Nipple Hee hee. Now A know y're not serious. St Paul's Church tower, hee hee.

Wick That's a laugh that'll rapidly commute across your face my friend. Ev'rything's ready.

Scrawdyke sits in his chair. Ingham sits to one side.

You stand in there. (*Indicates tea chest.*)

Nipple Why?

Scrawdyke Come on stand in there.

Nipple Oh Ai suppose Ai've got t' 'umour y'.

Wick sits down near the opposite end of the table from Ingham.

Scrawdyke Minister Blagden. As Minister of Justice and Prosecutor-General you will undertake the prosecution.

Wick Zealously, my leader.

Scrawdyke You will also place yourself at the disposal of the Prisoner should the Tribunal deem it necessary.

Wick Y' see, Nipple, ev'rything's fair and square. Y've got a Defence Counsel.

Nipple Y' can't 'ave the same man both prosecuting and defendin'. It's un'eard of.

Wick Oh no it isn't. Y've just 'eard of it.

Nipple Waarh. It wouldn't be allowed in a proper court.

Scrawdyke We're not int'rested in British legal procedure. This tribunal is constituted according to Dynamic Erectionist procedure.

Nipple What's that?

Wick You'll find out.

Scrawdyke stands.

Scrawdyke The Tribunal will rise.

Nipple Hee hee.

Scrawdyke On behalf of the Dynamic Erectionist Party, I hereby declare this Special Tribunal convened on the Sixth Day of Scrawdyke, Year One, in secret session, for the investigation of crimes against the Party, duly and legitimately open.

Wick Hail Scrawdyke!

Scrawdyke ⎫
Ingham ⎬ Hail Scrawdyke!

Nipple Hee hee.

Scrawdyke Dennis Charles Nipple, I charge you with Treason against the Party, entering into a Conspiracy with the Arch Enemy of the Party, Philip Allard, betraying your oath of allegiance, and generally being in league with the Forces of World Eunarchy.

Scrawdyke, Ingham and Nipple sit.

Nipple Ai must 'ave been very busy to 'ave done all that.

Wick 'Ow d' you plead? Guilty or Very Guilty?

Nipple Ai plead Not Guilty.

Wick There's no such plea.

Nipple That's ridiculous. Y' can't say Ai'm guilty before Ai've been tried.

Wick We can and do. This is a Dynamic Erectionist Tribunal. Y' can either plead Guilty or Very Guilty. You 'ave that choice.

Nipple That's noe choice.

Wick It is. And not only that it's your inalienable right.

Nipple Err, it's not fair.

Scrawdyke It's not the business of this Tribunal to be fair. Fairness doesn't enter into it. We're here to investigate the depth and scope of your crimes not whether they 'appened.

Wick It doesn't matter to us whether or not they did 'appen. The possibility that they might 'ave 'appened is sufficient. Even if you could prove conclusively that they did not, in fact, take place it wouldn't make any difference.

Scrawdyke I must say that it's my personal opinion that they didn't. But it's quite irrelevant.

Nipple Then 'ow –

Wick The fact we can conceive of them 'appenin' is sufficient.

Scrawdyke The existence of this Tribunal is your indictment.

Nipple Well in that case if Ai c'n conceive 'at you're capable of some crime it means you're guilty too.

Scrawdyke Certainly not.

Nipple Why?

Scrawdyke Because we're trying you. You're not trying us.

Wick Because we're calling the tune and you aren't. That gives us the right to be right.

Nipple Hee hee, if this wasn't a joke it'd be a surreal nightmare.

Wick The prisoner refused to take his case seriously and spoke flippantly.

Nipple Hee hee.

Wick Well 'ow d' y' plead?

Nipple Ai don't plead at all. Ai don't recognize this tribunal or whatever y' like t' call it.

Wick So y're pullin' the old Charles the First bit on us.

Nipple What d' y' mean?

Scrawdyke If 'e wants t' play at Charles the First let 'im. It's fairly well known 'ow Charles the First ended up.

Nipple Y've got the wrong king.

Wick Y' what?

Nipple It wasn't Charles the First it was Charles the Second.

Wick We'll just add that t' the list of charges. Distortin' 'istory for 'is own ends.

Scrawdyke 'E pleads Very Guilty.

Nipple Ai don't plead anything.

Wick That is construed as pleadin' Very Guilty.

Scrawdyke It is.

Wick I think in a case like this, a case as serious as this, an exceptional plea of Very Very Guilty should be allowed.

Scrawdyke The Tribunal grants your request.

Nipple Well if Ai'm so guilty, what's the point in tryin' me?

Wick We can't just let you get away with any old claim. You may be overstatin' y'r case. You may not be anywhere as guilty as you plead. We've got t' see whether you're coal-black or charcoal-grey. The safety and future of the Party depend on it.

95

Scrawdyke Minister of Propaganda, Justice and the Interior, Prosecutor-General, I call upon you to open the case for the prosecution.

Wick I call upon the witness, Irwin Ingham, to lay his deposition before the tribunal.

Ingham Eh?

Wick Witness Ingham, will you please tell us exactly what you saw and heard yesterday evening.

Ingham Oh – well – er – what um –

Wick Far be it from me to put words into your mouth. Just tell the Tribunal in your own words what you saw and heard.

Ingham Oh – aye – well – Well – I er – A mean they were up – an' um, an' 'e said er – what it was like, an' y' see I'd been walkin', A mean A was walkin', just by there, an' as A was walkin' A saw like 'em, y' know, like goin' in, like goin' into it. Well I didn't know – A mean I didn't know – then, y' know, er – Well, A mean, A wondered. So, like, as A say, they went – A mean they went in, an' then, well, A suppose they went up. Well one at a time – like – A mean that's what – And anyway, as A say, one went up, one of 'em, then – then the other like and er – And anyway when they'd – when they'd gone up, gone in, y' know, an' they'd well, they'd got there, got up there, to the top of – y' know, where it er – was – Well – they met A suppose. A mean like they did like – Then, then when they were – this – well they er – A mean they er – to each. A mean when they went in, when they first went in, when one went in an' then the other, 'e went in, well then I went, I went in, y' know because it just seemed a bit – Anyway, so, as A say, I went – I followed, A suppose y' might say, that, an' A saw 'em go, through this – an' then go up – an' I – an' when I, A mean when I got – they were er – y' know, An' when

96

they'd finished well, they came, they came down. They came down an' went out, an' then I came down an' I went out. A mean after they'd come down, come out, gone down, come out, I'd gone, A mean come, A mean out – I'd, well, y' know – An' so really that's er – what I c'n, y' know, that's just er – that is what, well, y' know – that's it.

Wick Thank you. So there you are. Conclusive testimony on the part of an eyewitness.

Nipple Waah. 'E didn't –

Scrawdyke Silence! The prisoner is not permitted to speak at this juncture.

Wick So there we 'ave it in all its disgustin' detail. You were seen entering St Paul's Church, climbing the tower, and up there on the ledge, you were overheard conspiring with the Arch Eunuch, and Enemy of the Party, Philip Allard, whom you had previously arranged to meet there by phone. You informed him of all the Party's secret plans in return for a glossy picture-book of Tahitian nudes and your picture in the '*Uddersfield Daily Examiner*. I submit that the case is fully proved against the enemy of the Party, Dennis Charles Nipple.

Scrawdyke I now call upon the Minister of Justice and Prosecutor-General to open the case for the defence.

Nipple Ai'll conduct mai own defence.

Scrawdyke That can't be allowed. You'll be allowed an opportunity to speak at the proper time.

Nipple Waargh.

Wick The defence rests.

Nipple Waargh.

Scrawdyke The prisoner will now be allowed to confess.

Nipple What d' y' mean confess? Hee hee. Ai didn't even know y' could get up that church tower.

Wick Ignorance is no excuse.

Nipple Well Ai suppose y' must 'ave y' little games.

Scrawdyke I don't play games, Nipple. I never 'ave an' I never will. I've never played a game in my life, I hate games. I've always avoided 'em. I'll show you whether I'm playin' games. (*He rises.*)

Wick The Tribunal will rise.

Ingham and Nipple get up.

Nipple Waah.

Scrawdyke It is the sentence of this Tribunal that Dennis Charles Nipple shall firstly be expelled from the Party of Dynamic Erection. And that secondly he is sentenced to Death. The execution of the second part of this sentence not being practical in the present circumstances, is suspended until such time as it is practicable, whereupon it will be carried out summarily. It is my Decree as Leader of the Dynamic Erectionist Party that, until such time as the sentence can be executed, Dennis Charles Nipple shall be totally ostracized by all the members of the Party, that his name must not even be mentioned and that he be regarded as having ceased to exist except for the purpose of carrying out the sentence of Death.

Nipple looks round at the set faces.

Nipple But –

Wick Y're dead, Nipple. For all intents an' purposes y're now a corpse.

Nipple But y' must be – A mean y' can't really – Ai mean it's – Ai mean if y' really do, did – It'd mean – It'd mean y' were mad.

Scrawdyke I'm mad! I'm mad! Y' 'eard what 'e said, I'm mad! 'E sez I'm mad! That's really convincin' coming from you. It really rings true. The phantom novelist, the solipsist, the egoist, the surrealist figment of y'r own diseased imagination! The fantast 'oo c'n quite seriously arrange t' meet the 'eadmaster of an Art School on an icy ledge on the top of rickety church tower in a blizzard in the middle of winter – 'e says I'm mad! Y' just couldn't wait. Y' always 'ave t' be the centre. Y' can't submit y'r own perverted ego t' something bigger than y'self. You've betrayed me! Me personally! I brought you in. I trusted you, I gave you ev'rything. I give. I open, I trust, and you defecate on me as soon as – Well you'll find I have another side. I'll show you. I'll get you. You degenerate imbecile! I shan't forget. The day'll come. I'll hunt you down to the ends of the earth. I'll follow. I'll track. I'll make you wish you'd never been born. I could strangle you with my bare hands! I could drive a six-inch nail through your head! I've been too quick for you. I always am. I'm always in front. I always am. I always will be. I'll get you. I'll get you. I will I'll show, I'll –

He is shaking and speechless with rage. The other three are transfixed. Pause.

Nipple Y' mean it. (*Pause.*) But – why?

Scrawdyke Why? Because I!

Nipple Ai – Ai don't know why y' should want t' do this t' mee. Ai never did – an' y' know that, y' said that. Ai mean Ai can't see why it is y' – Ai've always 'ad – Ai've always resp – Ai've always 'ad an 'igh respect for you. Ai know we've 'ad our disagreements an' Ai've disagreed but – Ai can't see why y' want t' do this t' mee. Why should y'? Ai mean Ai've always thought you were a man, one man in this town 'oo was above, essentially above mere petty spite. Ai might not 'ave told y', 'ave said it to y', but then it's not mai nature. Ai don't find it easy. Is that what y' want? Y' want to see me grovel? Well if it is Ai'm not goin' t' say Ai'm not 'urt by what y've just said. Ai thought you were the only one 'oo – Ai valued our friendship. An' now y' want t' do this. – Oh come on, Mal, let me in on it, Ai know it's not a game, but tell me it's a re'earsal for some trial yoo intend to 'old in the future for some reel enemy of the party.

Scrawdyke It was your trial.

Nipple Y' really want me t' go? An' if y' could y'd really 'ave me killed?

Scrawdyke Yes!

Nipple Well – that's bad. That's really very bad. All these years and Ai thought you were mai friend. It's bad for mee but it's even worse for you. Ai feel sorry for y'.

Scrawdyke Get out of my sight!

Nipple All right

Wick And if you dare to say a word or write a word –

Nipple Don't worry! Ai've no desire t' write about you or anything t' do wi' y'. It's beneath me, unworthy of mee! (*He shuffles to the door and opens it.*) Ai go an' we shall never meet again. But Ai want y' to know that whyever and 'owever you've persecuted mee – Ai forgive you.

He goes out, closes the door. His slow tread is heard going down the stairs. The remaining three stand motionless.

Blackout

SCENE 10

Lights up. Ingham's sleeping-bag is stretched out on the floor. Ingham is lighting the gas ring. During the following he puts the kettle on and makes tea. Wick comes in.

Wick 'Ail Scrawdyke!

Ingham Oh aye. 'E's not 'ere.

Wick Where is 'e?

Ingham 'E's gone for a prowl round.

Wick Oh.

Ingham 'E likes that, prowlin' around.

Wick Aye. 'Ow d' y' kip?

Ingham Well A mean –

Wick Yeh.

Ingham A'm just mekkin' some tea.

Wick Great. There are six-foot drifts up our way.

Ingham Up Cowcliffe.

Wick Yeh. Ey listen. Me ma rang up Allard this mornin'.

Ingham Eh!

Wick Yeh. She wanted t' know why me grant 'adn't come through. I tried t' bluff 'er, y' know, sayin' it'd just been 'eld up or summat. But it didn't work an' this morning' she phoned 'im.

Ingham Oh. What 'appened?

Wick Oh t' 'ole bloody thing came out. Now she knows why I 'avn't been goin' int' Tech ev'ry mornin', she knows A'm not just preparin' me thesis at 'ome. Man she went spare, she gave me the full treatment, either beg Allard t' tek me back or never darken 'er doorstep again.

Ingham Oh just t' same as me mam.

Wick Aye.

Ingham Y' goin' t' move in 'ere then?

Wick Well –

Ingham Oh – it's the seventh now. Two days t' go –

Wick Listen, Irwin, y' know the plan for Friday, 'ow feasible d' y' think it is?

Ingham Well –

Wick Just between you an' me.

Ingham What just –

Wick Yeh, without – just between you an' me.

Ingham Well – A think there are, is, A mean it does present – certain difficulties.

Wick Exactly.

Ingham But it doesn't – A mean like the's nowt we c'n –

Wick There is, I 'avn't told y' what Allard said t' me mother. 'E said 'at if you an' me apologize to 'im 'e'd consider tekkin' us back an' gettin' us grants goin' again. But 'e said we 'ad t' do it tomorrow, Thursday, or it's no go.

Ingham But we –

Wick Look, I don't like the idea of crawlin' back t' that bastard any more 'an you do.

Ingham A wasn't thinkin' of 'im.

Wick Aye. Well. Don't worry about that. I'm not suggestin' we walk out on Mal, desert the party, 'course not. I still want it t' succeed as much as I ever did. I'm goin' t' suggest a change of tactics that's all.

Ingham Oh 'e'll never –

Wick It's for the good of the Party, man. This thing on Friday's too much of a one-shot risk.

Ingham It's tekken y' a long time t' see that.

Wick Well we all got carried away. Now's the time for realistic reappraisal.

Ingham Try tellin' Mal that.

Wick Y're too much afraid of 'im. I'll persuade 'im.

Ingham 'Oo's ever managed t' persuade Malcolm Scrawdyke except Malcolm Scrawdyke.

Wick Don't worry we've got a good case, I'll put it to 'im. Don't worry, 'e'll see it, don't worry.

Ingham Well A wish A could be so –

Wick Don't worry, Irwin. Let's 'ave some o' this witch piss. (*Pours tea.*) We've only missed a week down there. Less 'an that. (*Looking at Scrawdyke's self-portrait.*) Mal's not a painter.

Ingham I'd just started a litho, some fish, but they'll 'ave gone off by now.

Wick Be nice t' do some paintin' again.

Ingham Aye. A suppose A could get some more.

Wick Y' know, for NDD, they provide y' wi' new canvases.

Ingham Aye A know they –

Wick Nice virgin springy new canvases. It's a great feelin' when y' put y' brush on to a new canvas an' y' feel that life in it. Sends a ripple up y'r arm man.

Footsteps.

Ingham Oh A'm not lookin' forward t' this.

Wick Don't get flustered just be natural.

Ingham Well A – oh –

Scrawdyke comes in.

Wick Hail Scrawdyke!

Scrawdyke 'Ail Scrawdyke. Give us some o' that tea.

Ingham Oh yeh.

Scrawdyke No milk?

Ingham No.

Scrawdyke Ah! The's nowt like a cup o' tea! I've just been down t' St Paul's Street t' look over the snow situation.

Wick Oh yeh, very important. It's not too thick down there, is it?

Scrawdyke Nah it's not too thick. I made my way down there, I moved cautiously. I took great care not t' be seen. Allard 'as spies ev'rywhere, anybody might be an Allard spy. But I know 'ow t' slink through this town without bein' seen. All the loose stuff's been cleared off St Paul's, they've got cinders down. The rest o' the route's clear too. T' snow's there but it's been pressed down smooth an' tight. As I walked along the route I saw the irony, I saw us glidin' 'ere on Friday night over the Royal road they're keepin' clear to their own destruction.

Wick Oh well that's um – Listen, Mal, me an' Irwin 'ave been, well, lookin' at certain aspects of the plan from a few new angles.

Scrawdyke Well there's nothing I like better than a new angle.

Wick Yeh I know that. That's why –

Scrawdyke I'm always open to new ideas. Some men can't keep out germs or damp, I can't keep out new ideas.

Wick Sure I know that. That's why these new ideas are goin' t' make our success even more certain than it is now.

Scrawdyke sits in his chair.

Scrawdyke The day I can no longer take in a new idea is the day I shall climb down the nearest grate an' allow myself to be sluiced away with all the other refuse.

Wick An' I'll be there, with y'. We'll get flushed down t' Bradley Sewerage Works t'gether. We c'n compare notes an' share the sights. But, anyway listen –

Scrawdyke Fire away.

Wick Right. Well listen Mal, I've been thinkin' about the plan for Friday, Scrawdyke the ninth. Now first of all A want t' say, y' know, I still think it's a great idea. It's more than that, it's a magnificent idea, it's a stroke of genius. There can be no two ways about that, it's a magnificent idea, it's a great plan. An' A'm not knockin' it, get that clear, I'm not for a minute knockin' it. I'd never knock it. It could achieve ev'rything we want, it could do it in one stroke, A mean that's t' 'ole beauty o' it. But, an' I only say this after a great deal of thought, y' know, after lookin' at the 'ole question thoroughly, which as realistic revolutionaries we must do, A mean that's what you've always said and I'm the first to agree. A mean be clear about this, I'm with you over the Party and our aims up to the 'ilt. Don't think A'm wavering, not a bit. What A'm goin' t' suggest is only becos I'm committed, y' know, one hundred per cent, to the movement. An' what I say is only prompted by the desire that we should succeed an' by nothin' else. Now what A'm tryin' t' say is, there's only one thing wrong with the plan as it stands at the moment, not the actual plan itself, as I say if it worked out it'd be magnificent. No I'm not criticizin' it as a plan, I'm only sayin' that there's a risk, well perhaps not even that, but let's say a possibility that it could fail. Not through any blunder on our part, A mean that's inconceivable, but through some factor completely outside our control. Now I'm not afraid for personal reasons, neither is Irwin, we've put our all into this Party an' if necessary we'd lay down our lives for it. That's the ultimate sacrifice any conspirator accepts from the word go an' we don't shirk it. Whatever risks there are we're right at your side, ready t' take whatever comes. A mean let's not beat about the bush, y're a great man, a great Leader, and nobody appreciates that more than I do. An' it's becos of all this that I don't think we should stake ev'rything on one throw. It'd be a tragedy, a cataclysmic tragedy, if we were't t' stake the future of the Party, the future of the country even the future of the world, on one act, 'owever great, an' it misfired through no fault of ours. It's all a matter of timin'. It could be another Beer 'All Putsch of 1923. That put 'Itler back ten years. 'E tried too much too soon. We can learn from that mistake. We're more on the ball. So listen 'ere's the new idea. We play it really cool, really really cool. Irwin and I go down to Allard t'morra an' beg 'im t' take us back. We really lay it on for 'im so 'e thinks we're completely 'umiliated. Haha, y' know, we feed 'im all that crap about wantin' t' do Finals, realizin' we'd jeopardized our careers, 'at we've realized we 'ave responsibilities, t' parents, teachers, talent, society, the 'ole shit'ouse. 'I think we've grown up a little in the past few days, sir.'

We'll make tears run down 'is face. We'll completely
fool 'im. But the important thing is we'll be back inside,
we'll be able t' strike at 'im from the inside. An' get this,
y'll love this, we'll tell 'im we saw through you. We'll say
we've realized you're a complete shit. 'At you just tried to
get some lolly out of us an' when y' found out we were
skint y' ran out on us. But then, an' this's the clincher,
we'll say y're 'armless. Allard'll relax, 'e'll withdraw 'is
spies, 'e'll think it's all over, ev'rything's cosy in 'is neat
little world again. But we'll be down there an' you'll be
up 'ere. All the time we seem t' be quietly working, we'll
be watchin'. Ev'ry night you'll 'ave a detailed report on
all 'is movements. We'll be able t' find out 'is movements
months ahead. On any given day. An' all the time we can
build up our numbers, a few more members of the right
calibre could make things easier. We could get cells
started up all over. Bradford, Leeds, 'Alifax, Brig'ouse,
Batley, even further afield, so 'at when the moment
arrived they'd be ready t' sound the call in all those
towns. We'd be in a far better position than we are now.
All the time you'd be up 'ere drawin' the noose ever
tighter. Just think what a great sense of 'idden power
that'd give y'. With Allard off the alert y' could move
about quite freely. We'd put it round y'd settled down to
a quite normal existence. Ha we could even say y'd got
married. An' all the time we'd be preparing, drawin' the
noose tighter, with no risks 'owever remote. Then
suddenly, out of this calm will suddenly erect the penis of
our conspiracy!

Well, Mal, what d' y' think?

Eh, what d' y' think? – Come on, Mal, what d' y' think
of it? – It's a great plan. Now y've 'eard it, what d' y'
reckon? Come on, Mal, what d' y' think? (*Pause.*)

Scrawdyke Phht!

Blackout

SCENE 11

Lights up. Mid-afternoon. Wick sits dejectedly, a blanket round him. Ingham has his sleeping-bag round his legs. Scrawdyke is standing looking out of the window.

Scrawdyke Scrawdyke the ninth. Not long to go before zero hour. The Old Era is drawing towards its close.

Wick Oooo it's cold!

Ingham Seems t' get colder.

Wick A'm sure it's never been as cold as this before.

Ingham Aye. I'n't it time we 'ad this fire on again?

Scrawdyke No.

Ingham It's nearly three.

Scrawdyke Not until quarter past.

Wick T' last time we 'ad it on was one o'clock.

Scrawdyke Quarter of an hour every two hours.

Wick 'Ow d' y' get quarter past three then?

Scrawdyke We count from the last switchin' off.

Wick Switchin' on.

Scrawdyke Switchin' off.

Ingham Switchin' on.

Scrawdyke Switchin' off.

Wick When we 'ad it on at one –

Scrawdyke Quarter past, I –

Ingham No A think John's –

Wick Y' switched it on y'self at one, A remember, y' asked Irwin.

Ingham Aye that's –

Scrawdyke Well if what y' say – an' I don't – it was an oversight.

Wick Oh hell what's quarter of an –

Scrawdyke It's a matter of policy, a matter of plannin'. That shillin's got t' be conserved.

Ingham But now we're so near to – y' know – surely it doesn't like – A mean 'ow much money 'ave we?

Wick You're the Minister of Finance.

Ingham But 'e's got the money.

Scrawdyke As leader I ask for an' am allocated funds by you as Minister of Finance. I decide policy an' policy requires money. Your job is to keep account and find money.

Ingham Aye so it seems.

Wick 'Ow much 'ave we got?

Scrawdyke At this moment we 'ave two an' sixpence.

Wick Well look why can't we 'ave another bob for the gas? It's so cold we're all stiff –

Scrawdyke I never felt better, never felt –

Wick Well Irwin an' me are stiff. We don't want to be stiff when the time comes, we want to be supple and ready for –

Scrawdyke All right, lads. I've decided t' make a policy change. You two go over t' t' Gates Café an' get a shilling. Spend the other one and six as y' see fit. Get another bob for the gas, get a couple o' teas, whatever y' fancy. I delegate the decision to you. I step completely out of the situation and leave it all t' you.

Wick Right. come on, Irwin.

Ingham Aye.

Scrawdyke But make sure y're back 'ere in good time for zero hour.

Ingham Aren't you comin'?

Scrawdyke No.

Wick Come on.

They go out.

Scrawdyke Got rid of 'em for a while. Think a few things out. Let's 'ave this bloody fire on. I can 'ear 'em comin' up, turn it off. They'll never be able t' work out 'ow much the' was in it. An' if they do complain A'll tell 'em it's a faulty meter. Well it's been a near scrape lately. Yeh, but I've managed. I c'n keep 'em goin', but it's not goin' t' be – Oh what's goin' t' 'appen tonight? It's all nonsense just one long wank, that's all it is, from beginnin' to end. An' I'll never dare try, not even try! I'm so weak, no will, supine – I feel so ill, gnawin' in me stomach, constipated – Oh! What else is there now 'at Ann's –? I've got t' try, it doesn't matter 'at it can't succeed, it only matters 'at I lead – If only we do something it doesn't matter. I've just got to throw myself into it, do it without thought, in a trance. Yes, that's it. A trance is necessary for action. Just lead 'em through that blasted door – Yes, yes – Ooogh!

He huddles by the fire. Crouching down to it. The door opens quietly and Ann Gedge, in her early twenties, in

*an overcoat, a scarf round her head, comes in. She
stands just inside the door. Scrawdyke doesn't notice
her.*

Just act – act – that's it – Don't think – Act, act, yes – that's
(*He turns round and sees her.*) Wah!

*Scrawdyke jumps up. They stare at each other. Then
Ann closes the door and starts moving slowly round the
room examining its contents: the sink full of filthy pots,
the painted boards, the rubbish, the dustbin, the self-
portrait, etc. Ending up looking at the banner.
Scrawdyke watches her transfixed.*

Ann So – this is it.

Scrawdyke This is what?

Ann 3a Commercial Chambers.

Scrawdyke Oh. (*Pause.*)

Ann That's where y' sleep?

Scrawdyke Yes.

Ann Comfy?

Scrawdyke All right.

Ann Warm?

Scrawdyke Enough.

Ann Mm. 'Oos's the sleepin'-bag?

Scrawdyke Irwin's.

Ann 'E sleeps 'ere too?

Scrawdyke Yes.

Ann Y' all sleep 'ere?

Scrawdyke Yes.

Ann You eat up 'ere too?

Scrawdyke Sometimes.

Ann 'Oo cooks?

Scrawdyke 'Ooever –

Ann 'Ooever feels like it?

Scrawdyke 'Ooever's allocated to it.

Ann Oh. You don't do any.

Scrawdyke I didn't say I didn't.

Ann Y' do?

Scrawdyke When the need arises.

Ann What d' y' cook?

Scrawdyke Well –

Ann What d' y' make?

Scrawdyke The usual things

Ann Such as.

Scrawdyke Well, such as – just the usual –

Ann Nothing fancy.

Scrawdyke Certainly not.

Ann Just good solid plain stuff?

Scrawdyke Yes.

Ann 'Oo's the best cook?

Scrawdyke What?

Ann 'Oo's the best cook?

Scrawdyke Well – we're all more or less the same.

Ann But you c'n 'old y'r own?

Scrawdyke I c'n wield a pan.

Ann When the need arises.

Scrawdyke Yes.

Ann An' y' cook on that?

Scrawdyke Yes.

Ann No stove.

Scrawdyke No.

Ann Where d' y' keep the utensils?

Scrawdyke Oh – around.

Ann Oh, y' keep 'em in the sink. (*She lifts a battered filthy pan out of the sink.*) Heinz Spaghetti. Burnt. 'Oo does the washin' up?

Scrawdyke Nobody.

Ann Y' still believe in fairies.

Scrawdyke If we want a cup or a plate we just douse it off. We don't make a song and dance out if it.

Ann A song an' a dance wi' a cup an' a plate. Sounds entertainin'.

Scrawdyke Well we don't go in for it. I don't concern myself with things like that.

Ann And this is the banner. Mm. (*She sits in Scrawdyke's chair. Pause.*)

Scrawdyke Erm – erm – y're er – Y've just er – come from Tech?

Ann Mm.

Scrawdyke Oh – Y' didn't 'ave an evenin' class t'night?

Ann nods.

Oh – so you er – you er – decided to um – come away?

Ann Huhuh.

Scrawdyke An' you er – you er –

Ann I came 'ere. (*She gets out cigarettes, lights herself one.*) 'Ave a fag.

Scrawdyke Oh – ta. (*Pause.*)

Ann I saw you on Monday night.

Scrawdyke Where?

Ann Walkin' past t' Co-op.

Scrawdyke Oh.

Ann I was waitin' for t' trolley.

Scrawdyke Oh, well. A didn't see y'.

Ann A thought y' might 'ave done.

Scrawdyke No, no, A didn't.

Ann A thought it was funny –

Scrawdyke A didn't see y'.

Ann – A mean if y'd seen me –

Scrawdyke A didn't.

Ann – y'd 'ave stopped.

Scrawdyke Oh yeh, yeh, if A'd seen y'.

Ann But y' didn't?

Scrawdyke No A didn't.

114

Ann 'S funny A thought for a moment y' 'ad.

Scrawdyke No A didn't.

Ann Y' just seemed to look in my direction.

Scrawdyke Well A didn't.

Ann A realize that now.

Scrawdyke No I didn't see y'. I was in an 'urry.

Ann Oh well it's just one o' those things. Where are the others?

Scrawdyke Oh – er – they're out on a mission.

Ann Connected with the – ?

Scrawdyke Yes.

Ann Oh. A thought A saw 'em goin' int' t' Gates.

Scrawdyke Well – that's where they 'ave t' make a contact.

Ann Ah. Y're still goin' t' do it then?

Scrawdyke Of course we are.

Ann An' y're still sure it'll succeed?

Scrawdyke It can't fail.

Ann It's tonight?

Scrawdyke Yes. Ey you 'aven't?

Ann 'Course not.

Scrawdyke We can't be too careful. We move with stealth.

Ann That fire doesn't give much off.

Scrawdyke I don't notice the cold.

Ann 'S just as well. (*Pause.*) 'Ow would you like t' shaft me?

Scrawdyke Eh!

Ann I said 'ow would you like to shaft me.

Scrawdyke Buh –!

Ann It's a simple enough question. 'Ow would you like t' 'ave sexual intercourse with me?

Scrawdyke is speechless.

Either y' would or y' wouldn't.

Scrawdyke I – I – I –

Ann I don't see any difficulties. It seems quite straightforward t' me. I thought y'd prided y'self on y'r rapid perception.

Scrawdyke I've never 'eard –

Ann I know that. That's why A asked y'.

Scrawdyke I don't know 'ow y' dare ask such a question.

Ann I dare becos there's not the slightest chance of it ever 'appenin'.

Scrawdyke Y' don't just – just – it's disgustin'.

Ann What's disgustin' about it?

Scrawdyke Well it's a – it's a –

Ann An' you're the man 'oo prides 'imself on 'is brutal frankness!

Scrawdyke I'm frank when I need t' be. It's all a question of context.

Ann It's all a question of whether it's Malcolm Scrawdyke 'oo's bein' frank or somebody else.

Scrawdyke I'd never say what you've just said to any woman.

Ann Only becos y'd never dare.

Scrawdyke Becos I've got a – I've got a proper sense of propriety.

Ann Well this's a role I never expected. Don't tell me the's a Victorian gentleman lurking beneath all that angry young muck.

Scrawdyke Nobody speaks t' me like –

Ann That's the trouble. Nobody dare. Y've got the biggest front – I wouldn't 'ave dared either if A 'adn't seen what there is be'ind it. There I was for months in awe of y', just like all t' rest, not darin' t' so much as ask y' what time it was. Dreamin' about the day when the great man might stoop down from 'is 'ights an' deign t' speak t' me. Huh, t' think I used t' think you must 'ave a diff'rent woman ev'ry night o' t' week if y' wanted to. I asked about y', never mind 'oo, an' nobody knew anything about it. So I could only think y' weren't int'rested or none o' t' women in 'Uddersfield came up t' y'r demands. An' so A screwed up courage. I screwed up my nerve t' ask you! An' when y' grunted, when y' grunted 'Yeh' A couldn't believe it, A thought y' must be puttin' on an act for my benefit. So we went out an' I was – well, surprised at first. Then I thought, well 'e's a bit shy, 'e's not used to it after all, so I'll 'elp 'im along a bit. A bit! An' then I realized the big secret. The great man's scared stiff of anything in knickers! Y're the biggest virgin outside a convent. Y're right, girls don't usually talk like this, They don't need to. I don't make an 'abit of it. But the's no future in being subtle with you.

Scrawdyke The 'ole thing's just a vast misconception on your part.

Ann Is it!

Scrawdyke Yes it is. I never looked twice in the way you mean. I never looked twice at y'.

Ann That's true, y' didn't even dare look.

Scrawdyke I didn't want to.

Ann Then why did y' go out with me?

Scrawdyke I'm gregarious.

Ann An' what were y' doin' 'angin' about down near our 'ouse?

Scrawdyke I told y' –

Ann Ah A know what y' told me. An' what were y' doin' 'angin' around my bus stop?

Scrawdyke I was just walkin' past.

Ann A know that's what y' did. I'm talkin' about what y' wanted t' do.

Scrawdyke 'Ow d' you know what I wanted t' do?

Ann I've got a magic eye 'at sees straight through little men like you.

Scrawdyke Don't call me a little man.

Ann In spite of the beard an' long scruffy 'air.

Scrawdyke I don't waste my time on hair!

Ann It doesn't waste its time on you.

Scrawdyke It grows where it should in the way that it should. I know what it's up to. I leave it alone. Show me a well-groomed 'ead and I'll show you an enemy of the creative imagination.

Ann A beautiful thought never came from a beautiful 'ead. Y're the daftest man A've ever met.

Scrawdyke I'm not going t' waste my time talkin' about 'air.

Ann Y' prefer t' waste y' time in other ways.

Scrawdyke You can't see –

Ann Never mind what A can't see. Let me tell y' what A can. I see three timid little men. One 'oo leads the other two along becos 'e's got a louder voice that's all, an' fills 'em up wi' big ideas of 'emselves. One 'oo's very quick at ev'rything but standin' up for 'imself. 'E's another great lover. I once caught cold waiting for 'im t' make a move in a freezin' yard. And a third – well, 'e's only ever anywhere becos 'e's not somewhere else.

Scrawdyke grins.

A see y' recognize these descriptions.

Scrawdyke I 'ave a taste for caricature.

Ann Well these three supermen are goin' t' pinch a paintin' from a completely unguarded art gallery, they're goin' t' sneak up be'ind a completely unsuspectin' 'eadmaster an' clout 'im over the 'ead. Then they're goin' t' blackmail 'im by threatenin' t' expose the fact that 'e kissed a girl student under t' mistletoe at a Chris'mas party unless 'e's prepared t' smash up the paintin' they've pinched. Then they're goin' t' break their promise to 'im an' tell ev'rybody what a rotter he is. Then ev'rybody'll see what great big 'eroes they all are. This's the great scheme these three giant brains 'ave been buildin' up over the last week. But Allard's worth ten of 'em.

Scrawdyke So that's what y' came up 'ere for. Allard's worth ten of us is 'e! Well you'll see. Now I know 'oo's side you're on.

Ann Oh don't be silly. I've no special love for Allard. 'E tends t' bully sometimes, an' the way 'e tried t' ostracize you was very bad, but 'e's not a bad man, 'e does 'is best. The thing is, 'e goes the wrong way about it. A feel rather sorry for 'im really –

Scrawdyke Sorry for 'im! Sorry for that bastard! That's the last thing y' should be. There should be no pity for a ruthless, scheming, maniac like 'im. 'E should be regarded as a rabid vicious animal, the slightest flicker of sympathy and 'e'll be at y'r throat. That's exactly what 'e wants. Pity to 'im is weakness. 'E 'as no normal 'uman feelings. 'E's a monster. A completely separate species. A stinking accretion that pollutes ev'rything merely by its existence. The only thing t' do with – filth like that, the only course open, is to hack it to pieces!

Ann D' y' know 'oo y're talkin' about! D' y' really know 'oo y're – D' y' know what y're sayin'?

Scrawdyke I always know exactly what I'm sayin'.

Ann I 'ope y' don't. For your sake I –

Scrawdyke What d' y' mean for my sake!

Ann A mean if y' really believe all this twisted – then there's no 'ope for y'. That's why I came. Can't y' see what – I mean if y' can't be stopped –

Scrawdyke Ah stopped! Oh yes. Whatever it is I might want t' do, I've always got t' be stopped –

Ann Oh I don't mean in that way. Can't y' see, y' silly bugger what I – I mean stopped thinkin' all this, stopped bein' all this. All this twisted nonsense. All this pretence at bein' something y're not an' shouldn't ever want t' be. All this great man stuff 'at wouldn't be a great man even if it was. A mean even if y' were it. It's all wrong it's all sick. A don't know – But I feel y' could be – Y' must see 'at what A'm sayin' is true. Y' must know why I came. I came 'ere t' 'elp y'. I came 'ere t' 'elp y'. (*Pause.*)

Scrawdyke Y' came 'ere t' – (*Short pause.*)

Ann Yes.

Scrawdyke Well – 'ow – 'ow could you –?

Ann I don't know, Malcolm, it's for you –

Scrawdyke If – er, y' know, if – if –

Ann Mm. (*Pause.*)

Scrawdyke Oh no! Listen to you and I'd be finished. Reduced to a slack-mouthed nonentity, wanderin' about grinnin' at babies, sniffin' flowers, pattin' dogs on t' 'ead. Well that's not for me. I'm a man of a diff'rent stamp. When I'm angry I know 'at I'm alive, my blood runs, I tingle, I am something.

   Footsteps on the stairs. Wick and Ingham come in.

Ingham Oh!

Wick Aye aye.

Ann 'Lo.

Wick What's all this then?

Ann A'm just goin'.

Wick Oh – Come up from Tech?

Ann Yeh. A was just on me way 'ome. A thought A'd pop in.

Wick Oh. 'Ow's Tech these days?

Ann Well – T' 'eatin' wasn't workin' properly until t'day. But a man came up an' got it rumblin' an' gurglin'.

Wick 'T sounds like a train comin' in.

Ingham Aye it does.

Ann Yeh.

Ingham A suppose like y' di'n't do Life t' first –

Ann No we couldn't.

Wick What d' y' do Costume Life instead?

Ann Yeh.

Scrawdyke Why don't y' ask 'er 'ow Mr Allard is?

Wick Eh?

Scrawdyke She's in the best possible position t' tell y' 'owt y' should care t' know about 'im becos she came 'ere straight from 'im.

Ann Oh really even –

Wick Ey! Is this true?

Ann Of course it's not!

Scrawdyke All right explain to 'em why y' came. I'll keep my mouth shut, I'll keep completely out of it. Never let it be said I tried t' prejudice y'r position.

Ann You bastard!

Scrawdyke Well that's goin' t' make a fine impression for a start.

Wick What y' doin' 'ere?

Ann Oh – I came t' try an' stop y', stop y' be'avin' like a bunch o' kids.

Wick 'Ow d' y' mean?

Ann Oh come off it, Wick.

Wick No. What d' y' mean?

Ann All this nonsense y've got cooked up for tonight –

Wick 'Ow d' y' know about that?

Ann 'Ow d' y' think! I was told about it.

Wick Told! 'Oo told –

Ann Your great leader 'imself told me.

Wick Mal?

Scrawdyke 'S quite true. I'll tell y' 'ow it 'appened. When she came through that door I was almost surprised. I immediately asked myself why. I flicked through the permutations an' I came up with the answer. She'd been sent as a spy. Why else should she come 'ere?

Ann Oh this's – I'm not listenin' to any more. (*She moves towards the door.*)

Scrawdyke Oh no we can't 'ave that. Straight down t' report t' Philip David Trevor.

Wick moves between Ann and the door, as yet unmenacingly.

Wick Yeh. Y' can't just shove off. There are things t' be explained.

Ann Oh it's obviously – You two believe ev'rything this bastard wants y' t' believe. Talk about suckers! I'm not goin' t' bother –

She moves again towards the door. Wick blocks her way.

Wick So we're suckers, are we?

Ann Let me pass.

Scrawdyke moves beside Wick.

Scrawdyke Oh no. She thinks we're goin' t' let 'er run out of 'ere, just like that.

Wick If we did then we should be suckers.

Ann Get out of the way, y' silly –

Scrawdyke We're only silly kids. We aren't capable of doin' anything.

Wick Is that so. Well, we'll 'ave t' try an' convince 'er otherwise.

> *Ann moves forward, she makes a gesture to push Wick out of the way, he gently pushes her off.*

P'raps this'll convince 'er.

Ann Now look, don't be –

Scrawdyke It's beginnin' t' dawn. P'raps we aren't playin'.

Wick She's beginnin' t' get a bit anxious.

Ann Oh don't be ridiculous. Now come –

Scrawdyke She's not sure now. P'raps we aren't just things after all.

> *They start to move towards her, she backs away.*

Wick She speaks with contempt but she backs away.

Scrawdyke We aren't men she says but she's a woman.

> *Ann moves farther away as they slowly approach her.*

Wick An' she's all alone with us up 'ere.

Scrawdyke Outside the snow muffles all sound.

Wick There's nobody in the buildin'.

Scrawdyke She's weak an' warm an' frightened.

> *Ingham starts moving towards her too. She continues to back away.*

Ann All right, all right, you win, y've scared me, if that's what y' want.

Scrawdyke That's not what we want.

Wick We want more than that.

Scrawdyke We've got to show 'er what 'appens t' women 'oo pry.

Wick Show 'er what we can do.

Scrawdyke T' women 'oo treat men with contempt.

Ann Look, please.

Scrawdyke Ah! She starts to beg.

Wick She's terrified.

Scrawdyke She's quiverin'.

Wick She's waitin'.

Scrawdyke For their hands.

Wick On 'er warm soft body.

Scrawdyke Which must be punished, punished, punished –

Ann No, no, no, no, y' don't, now stop, please, enough's, no, no –

Wick Punished, punished, punished –

Ingham Punished, punished, punished –

Ann is too terrified now to speak. They are almost on her when Scrawdyke breaks into the dog howls we have heard in earlier scenes. The howls are immediately taken up by the other two. When they are only about a foot from her she suddenly leaps at them and tries to club her way through. She flails her arms and hits with her

*fists. They pounce on her violently, howling at the top
of their voices. She screams. They savagely beat her
down. Doubled up and under a rain of blows she tries
to escape their frenzy but only manages to get a little
way. Ingham seizes at her and tears her coat half off. A
blow from Wick across the face sends her reeling back.
All on top of her they beat her down relentlessly, she
crumples to the ground as the blows stun her.
Scrawdyke kicks her prostrate body. Their frenzy
abates, the howling ceases. She lies motionless. They
stand around her exhausted, panting. As they stand
there the realization of what they have done begins to
break through. Wick totters round her.*

Wick Oh!

*He kneels down to her, stares, then he pulls her face
round gently, listens, moves her arm which is completely
limp.*

Ey! – Ey! –

Scrawdyke What –

Wick Oh!

Scrawdyke Wha's –

Wick She's dead!

Scrawdyke Eh!

Ingham makes a little moaning sound.

Wick She's dead! We've killed 'er. She's dead!

*Slowly they draw back from the body. They are
stunned. Scrawdyke sinks down on to a box, crumples
and moans. The others watch him and wait. Then:*

Ingham Mal! What – what –

Scrawdyke is oblivious to their questions.

Wick What are we goin' t' do? – What are we goin' t' do, Mal?

Slowly the girl starts to come round. They watch her, transfixed with horror. She dazedly stumbles to her feet, looks around wild-eyed, then retching, staggers across the room and through the door. We hear her stumbling down the stairs. Silence. Scrawdyke pulls himself together.

Scrawdyke Tergiversator! The whole thing was feigned. The whole thing was nothing but another trick! We ought to 'ave been more thorough. She ought to 'ave been dead. She deserved it. You seemed abashed, you seemed disconsolate. We mustn't be abashed by things like this. We must steel ourselves. It's them or us. Remember that. It's those 'oo strike first. Do you think she'd 'ave 'esitated for a minute, for a second, if she'd been the stronger? Oh no! I know 'ow y' felt, lads, the first time. We're too humane that's our trouble, it does us credit. I had a suspicion all along that she was feigning. But I didn't let on. Do you know why? I'll tell you why. There's a streak of weakness, of sentimentality, in all of us. It's got to be recognized, it's got to be wrestled with. It's got to be brought out into the open. It needs the right incident to entice it out. I used this incident. I let it come out. I gave it full play. I let it suffuse me. So that once and for all time, with utter finality, I could reject it. That's the way to handle temptations. Every saint knew that, let 'em roll then smack 'em down. Well I smacked mine down. I was just on the verge of giving mine the chop when she shoved off. Another second and I was goin t' say: 'Hack up the body.' Never mind, there'll be other opportunities. What we've just done makes the putsch even more urgent. If we don't act decisively now our destruction of her threat will have been in vain. We shall have done it all for nothing. Have we been through so much, suffered such privations, been goaded to such extremities for nothing? We most certainly have not. We are about to leap from our corner at the throat of the world! And then we shall see who cries for mercy, and then we shall see who begs for it, and then we shall see who gets it! We are the Arbiters of the Future! (*Short pause.*)

Wick Yeh, well, we'd better get ready.

Ingham Aye A suppose so. (*He gets the portfolio.*)

Scrawdyke When the time comes, Act, Act, don't think, Act.

Ingham 'Ow long is there t' go?

Scrawdyke is now standing still.

Scrawdyke One minute.

Wick Well this is it.

Ingham Seemin'ly so. (*He puts the portfolio under his arm.*)

Wick I avn't made a will.

Scrawdyke Thirty seconds – twenty – fifteen – five – one.

Scrawdyke stands where he is. The others stand where they are, watching him, absolutely motionless. The pause must be held for as long as possible. Then suddenly –

Wick We're not goin' t' do it! We're not goin' t' do it! After all the noise from 'im, after what 'e's just made us do t' that bird, after what 'e's just said, when the moment arrives 'e 'asn't got the nerve t' do it. Look at 'im – like a bloody statue! Petrified! Oh this's the biggest comedown I've ever – Oh after all the crap! We're ready t' foller 'im through that door. All we're waitin' for is 'is say so. An' 'e can't make it! The 'ole bloody thing was wind! The Great Leader, that miserable lump of solidified crap transfixed there!

Scrawdyke moves.

Scrawdyke So I couldn't –

Wick All this for nothing! Well this's the end.

Scrawdyke Well I didn't notice you jumpin' into action.

Wick I was waitin' for you. You were the Great Leader.

Scrawdyke Yeh waitin' for me as always.

Wick It was all y'r idea. You made us!

Scrawdyke With what – a gun?

Wick With y' bloody words. With all y' lies. Well y'r spell's broken. An' I'm goin' t' make sure it stays that way.

Scrawdyke Ah y're goin' t' kill me.

Wick I'm goin' t' tell people what you are. Then they'll know!

Scrawdyke I know you.

Wick I'm gettin' out o' this freezin' 'ole. I'm off through that door an' A'm not comin' back. You bastard y've ruined my life!

Scrawdyke Well at least I've achieved something.

Wick Nobody's listenin'. Come on, Irwin.

Ingham shakes his head.

Y're not stayin' 'ere after –

Ingham shrugs.

129

Aargh y' must be –

Scrawdyke Go on crawl away –

Wick Nobody's listenin'. (*He goes out, slams door. His feet are heard running down the stairs.*)

Scrawdyke What a turd! Good riddance! I ought to 'ave known better than to – Well you 'aven't said owt as usual. I know what y' think. Go on say it, y' might as well.

Ingham Well, Mal – A don't think as 'ow we can put it all on t' you. A don't think 'at what John said – We di'n't 'ave t' go along like, we di'n't 'ave to listen. A mean if we're goin' t' start talkin' about 'oo's to blame, 'oo's the worst one like, y' know, well A reckon, A reckon as y' could say I was, I am. A mean whereas you an' Wick, like, seemed t' 'ave, well – some genuine belief like, in what we were goin' t' do an' 'ow feasible it might be, well, y' see, I never did. I knew all along, like, from when y' suggested it, as 'ow it couldn't really work, an' as 'ow – well, y'd invented a lot of it. A mean A know y' – But anyway A just went on, A kept me mouth shut, A joined in – So really, y' could say like, 'at I'm the one 'oo –

Scrawdyke Nah. I instigated it. I'm not goin' t' – Anyway y're 'onest, Irwin. 'Ere 'ave a fag.

Ingham Ta.

Scrawdyke Just three left. That's all we got t' show for t' 'ole campaign. Three fags.

Ingham Well –

Scrawdyke Aargh if only I'd 'ad the nerve!

Ingham No – it was a good thing y' couldn't.

Scrawdyke P'raps y're right. P'raps it wasn't just a failure of nerve. P'raps it was some kind of warning message sent up from me subconscious. Some kind of switch thrown down there t' stop me. An inner sense of realism stepped in at the last moment and struck me rigid. I knew all along the thing wasn't feasible but I got carried away, pinned ev'rything to it, papered over the cracks. Lookin' back I can see all the mistakes. I should never 'ave tried t' use people like Wick an' Nipple. Inferior material. I shouldn't 'ave tried t' do it so quickly, I should 'ave got funds, got backin', got organs. Listen, Irwin, it's you an' me now. Let's pack this town in, get out, there's nothing 'ere. Let's get down London. That's where it all is. That's where they all are, millions of 'em. All the dissatisfied, waitin'. We can start all over again, right from scratch. We'll get jobs, build up some money, build up the 'ole thing slowly, meet people. I know you didn't agree with the old aims, well we'll work out new ones, a completely new set, together. We'll 'ammer 'em out as equals, y' can 'ave a veto, we'll be joint Leaders. If I open my big trap too much y' can tell me t' shut it. I won't speak without your permission. It'll be you an' me –

Ingham No! Mal, no.

Scrawdyke But what is there 'ere for you! Crawl back to Allard. 'E won't 'ave y' back. An' what's left? Some mis'rable job – tintin' snapshots.

Ingham Well if that's what it is that's what it'll 'ave t' be. It's no good, Mal, A know y' too well. An' it's not just that, even if ev'rything y' say could – Well A'm not cut out for it.

Scrawdyke Well –

Ingham All this power stuff. A mean even if I 'ave 'ad – certain – at times – Well A don't think like I ought to 'ave –

Scrawdyke Oh I know what y' mean. Y' think 'at certain

things we did were – wrong. Even bad. Well there is something in –

Ingham It's no use, Mal, whatever y' say. A'm not 'avin' owt t' do wi' parties an' movements an' erections, whatever y' say.

Scrawdyke The answer's no?

Ingham The answer's no.

Scrawdyke So after twenty-five years y've finally made a decision.

Ingham It seems so.

Scrawdyke I never thought I'd live t' see it.

Ingham Come t' that, nor did I.

Scrawdyke Well – well – good for you. Well go on then, piss off if that's what y' want.

Ingham Oh well just becos A'm not joinin' any more movements doesn't mean like –

Scrawdyke We can't remain friends.

Ingham Aye.

Scrawdyke That's no use t' me. Y're runnin' out on me like all the rest.

Ingham No A'm not.

Scrawdyke 'Course you are. So get on with it!

Ingham Well if that's – (*Pause.*) What y' goin' t' do?

Scrawdyke Mind y'r own business!

Ingham The's no need t' be like that. No, A mean seriously, what a' y' goin' t' do?

Scrawdyke What the 'ell d' y' think A'm goin' to do?

132

Ingham Well, A suppose mebbe go down London.

Scrawdyke Go down London. A lot o' good that's goin' t' do me.

Ingham Y' just said –

Scrawdyke If the's one thing I can do without it's somebody t' tell me what I've just said.

Ingham Well what'll y' do then?

Scrawdyke What can I do?

Ingham Mebbe tek a job?

Scrawdyke I've never done an honest day's work in me life an' I don't intend t' start now.

Ingham Well if y' don't, A mean, what –

Scrawdyke What can I do? There isn't anything I can do. I've no way to turn. I'm a complete and utter failure. I can't do anything, I've no resources. I'm finished. There's only one logical endin' t' this 'ole idiotic drama.

Ingham What's that?

Scrawdyke What do y' think it is? If I've nothing t' live for.

Ingham Oh don't talk like that. A mean even if y' don't mean it don't talk like that.

Scrawdyke When life becomes completely meaningless an' y' can't move in any direction.

Ingham Oh if y' really mean it y' wouldn't talk about it.

Scrawdyke I talk about ev'rything.

Ingham If A thought y' really meant it A'd stay like, A mean for t'night.

Scrawdyke Oh no, y' won't, go on get out.

Ingham Well –

Scrawdyke Go on!

Ingham Right. A'll just get me sleepin'-bag. (*He goes and gets it, rolls it up*.) Er, look, Mal.

Scrawdyke Get out! Tek y' bag an' piss off!

Ingham finishes tucking up his sleeping-bag and goes out. The door closes. His feet plod down the stairs. Silence.

Well that's it. The last of 'em gone. 'Ere I am, alone, empty, nothing! If only I – Oh! I'm not a person, I don't amount – I can't function on any level. They'll all be all right, they all live lives of their own in some way. As Irwin trudges 'ome through t' snow 'e is something, 'e 'as authenticity. 'E'll go on, get a menial job, find a bird, get married, 'owever inadequate 'e'll keep goin', 'e'll 'ave an identity. Wick, well at least 'e's a painter, 'e 'as that, 'e'll crawl back down t' Allard, justify it becos of 'is talent, laugh an' joke, 'ide 'is weakness, an' generally get on with some kind of a living. Nipple, even Nipple 'as 'is fantasies, they're real fantasies, 'e believes in 'em, they give 'im something, they are 'im. 'E'll go on, self-contained, dreamin', talkin'. I can't even believe in my own fantasies! They'll all go on. Allard, Boocock, all the rest, they'll all get on with it. Except me! Except me! Oh I can't stand it. This! Ev'rything exists except me, ev'rything 'as an identity. These objects, these easels, these cups, this dustbin, they all flaunt me! There's only one logical – as I told Irwin. That's the obvious – no doubt about that. But I couldn't even – But if I could. If there was a simple, quick – 'Ow could I do it? 'Ow could I? Gas? Well that's out for a start. Poison? Painless no violence. What could I poison meself with? Paint, squeeze a tube down me throat? Ugh no! Old tea leaves. Tannin? No just give y' cramps. Swaller a lump o' wood? Mouldy bread? We 'aven't any. Suck the dye out of me coat? Fluff? Fluff kills cats. Nah! – Smother y'self? Put y'r 'ead under a pillow an' press. No that's not a do-it-yourself method, y've got t' 'ave pressure. Put y'r 'ead through t' doorway and pull it shut. Snap? Oh don't be – I could throw meself out o' t' winder. (*Goes to window*.) Aaar can't get it open. Too small t' get through anyway. 'Ang meself. From what? Aaargh this place isn't designed for suicide. Go out. Under a bus? They move too slowly in this – Bury y'self in a drift? No no it's got t' be quick, no predetermination. A knife? (*Rummages about*.) Where – We 'ad a knife – What's this? A spoon! All we've got are spoons. Y' can't do away with y'self with a spoon! We 'ad a – 'Ere's a fork. 'T's got prongs, I suppose they'd go in. All right. Where? Soft part. Belly. Back. No can't push it in there. Where's soft an' vital? Buttocks. No wouldn't even be able to sit down after – What after? There mustn't be an after. That's the 'ole bloody – 'Eart! That's it. Get that. Where is it? Right side? Left side? Where? Where? Left, yes left. It's 'ard there. Through the ribs that's 'ow they do it. Feel there. Now get it ready. Close y're eyes. An' – Ugh! (*He staggers about gasping and falls to the floor*.) Very fittin'! A phoney suicide to end a phoney drama. A travesty of a death to finish off a travesty of a life. I'm still 'ere, I'm still 'ere! Oh I can't stand this silence. Let's – Music. (*Jumps up. Goes to tape recorder, switches it on, runs tape back a little, stops it. 'Hail Scrawdyke, Hail Scrawdyke –' booms out of it. He stands for a moment then switches it off*.) Oh what am I goin' t' do! I should 'ave a mental breakdown. That's what this should be. I should collapse, let 'em carry me away. Aar I can't even manage that. Even a mental breakdown needs more willpower than I've got. Why am I like – Oh Ann, she came 'ere to save me, I could 'ave – I could 'ave – what? I know there's another side. A warm dimension. What did we do! What did I – It was the act of animals. – Oogh! I can't stand it. I can't. There's nothing I can do. No way I – Ring Ann up. Apologize! Oh don't be absurd. Of all the things I've ever it's the most impossible. But if I could, I mean how – I mean if –

Scrawdyke paces up and down through a rapid and subtle light change which denotes the night passing. When the morning light is growing he sits in his chair. Full morning light. He looks at his watch. He is completely calm, drained, objective.

Nearly ten. Well it's nearly it. I know what I'm going t' do. As soon as it's ten, I'll walk through that door, go down the stairs, walk across the top o' Chapel 'Ill, through the snow, go into one o' the kiosks opposite, dial Ann's number. If 'er mother answers I'll ask for 'er. When she comes I'll say:

Hallo, this is Malcolm Scrawdyke, please don't ring off. I know how you feel but please listen. I want to apologize. I know that words can't begin to make up for what I did, I'm not trying to excuse it, there is no excuse. I just want you to know that I'm deeply ashamed. No words can express how disgusted I am with myself. I'm not asking you to forgive me. What I did was unforgivable. I don't even expect you to believe me. I simply wanted to try and tell you that I shall never forgive myself. (*He gets up and goes to window.*) Right. the kiosk's empty. (*Looks at watch.*) Fifteen – ten – five – two – Right.

He walks across the room, goes through the door, closes it behind him. His footsteps are heard going down the stairs. Silence. The light slowly fades out on the empty room.

The end